Without Prejudice

—the formal phrase ordained by custom (and required by the Marine Surveying Manual of the United States Salvage Association) to precede the surveyor's signature on any report he may file. In the same spirit as the more cumbersome formulae "Without fear or favor" and "the whole truth and nothing but the truth," it attests the marine surveyor's professional integrity and impartiality.

Without Prejudice

A History Of The
United States Salvage Association, Inc.
1921-1971

By

C. BRADFORD MITCHELL

To Louise

WHO STOOD BY

ACKNOWLEDGMENTS

THE thanks owed by the writer of any book are almost illimitable. Parents, family, teachers, professional colleagues, and friends of every vintage have made their contributions, which should be acknowledged. However, to protect the book from being thus crowded out of its covers, it is usual to mention in print only the recent assistance without which *this particular* book would not have come to birth. To anyone who has lent such assistance, yet been forgetfully omitted from the ensuing list, I extend, besides profound apologies, the assurance that he is in some of the finest company I have known.

Unstinted appreciation goes to the following, who reviewed and commented most helpfully on all or a major part of the manuscript: Percy Chubb, II, Clifford G. Cornwell, Captain Jones F. Devlin, Jr., Robert R. Dwelly, W. Bradford Harwood, Emil A. Kratovil, Walter E. Maloney, Esq., Gilbert B. Oxford, and J. Paul Thompson.

The following gave generously of their time and knowledge through interviews, telephone conversations, lengthy letters, picture and data research, or partial review of the text: Charles A. Auld, Peter S. Barracca, Frank O. Braynard, Max L. Brown, John S. Bull, Joseph A. Cerina, Mrs. George Anne Daly, Mrs. Beatrice Dobbins, Edward F. Ganly, Captain Richard D. Gatewood, USN (ret), Larry Guerin, William S. Henry, Harold Jackson, S. Donald Livingston, John B. McCubbin, Esq., Charles J. Monaghan, Rear Admiral Edmond J. Moran, USNR (ret), E. P. Pulliam, Rear Admiral Halert C. Shepheard, USCG (ret), James C. Sherman, Andrew S. Varni, William F. Watkins, and Commander Arthur E. Wills, USN (ret).

Finally, there are few of the present United States Salvage Association family—executive, professional, or clerical; at headquarters or in the field—to whom I am not lastingly indebted, directly or indirectly, for aid and friendly encouragement in the completion of this history. Working with them has been a privilege.

C. BRADFORD MITCHELL

North Woodstock, New Hampshire
September, 1971

TABLE OF CONTENTS

PROLOGUE

A CONFERENCE ON THE NEW YORK EXPRESS

THE time was the spring of 1920, and life was leisurely, as man has since come to measure motion. London might already have been bombed from the air, and the Atlantic spanned by plane, but the four-o'clock shuttle and the executive jet were as undreamed-of as Apollo XV. The coat of arms of the traveling businessman was still flanked by those heraldic creatures of latter-day mythology, the iron horse and the ocean greyhound.

On the afternoon of April 10 a group of men whose business concerned ships were returning to New York from Washington by train. Gathered in the club car, they were reviewing the mission which had taken them to Capitol Hill that day: the presentation to Congress and the United States Shipping Board of a plan to revive and expand American ocean hull insurance in support of the Government's program to revive and expand the nation's merchant marine.

Without serious exaggeration, the group might have been called the strategic high command of marine underwriting in the United States. It included Benjamin Rush, handsome and aristocratically groomed, with an incisiveness sometimes verging on the abrupt; William H. McGee, short and rotund, whose geniality masked his extraordinary fund of analytic shrewdness; and Walter Wood Parsons, thoughtful and dignified, admired as an underwriter even by those who found him overly prim and positive. Also present were three fire insurance executives, comparative newcomers to the ocean marine business: Louis F. Burke, Edwin C. Jameson, and Gomer H. Rees. Each of the six was a president or vice president of a leading national insurance firm, and a member of the underwriters' committee which on behalf of fifty American companies had drawn the blueprints for the American Marine Insurance Syndicates just submitted to the House Merchant Marine and Fisheries Committee.

One colleague of comparable stature, diplomatic but forceful New Englander William R. Hedge, was not with them—though he had been earlier, as a result of a mixup which had been the most vexatious feature of a generally successful day. Since the trip's purpose was mainly ceremonial, it had not been thought necessary that Hedge break off his vacation in Pinehurst, North Carolina, to come to Washington, and he had been so advised by telegram from committee counsel. But the vital "not" had been lost from this message in transmission; hence a somewhat disgruntled Hedge, after a superfluous visit to the capital, was now on a train speeding in the opposite direction.

On the New York train, the center of the group at the moment was counsel whose negative adverb had been mislaid, and who had just been instructed to notify Hedge that the committee would reimburse his wasted travel expenses, if not his lost vacation time. Archibald G. Thacher, Esq., had been legal adviser to marine insurance organizations for a decade. He was an erect man of rather severe appearance—a commanding mien, as it would then have been called—which made his universally-employed title of "Major" seem natural and fitting. To a very considerable degree the syndicate blueprints just deposited in Washington reflected his draftsmanship. Now, before they had even received formal government approval, and over seven weeks before they were to be translated into a working mechanism, he had an amendment to propose.

As he reported it in a letter to Hedge from New York that evening, "I suggested to the other members of the Committee the importance, in my judgment, of at once taking steps to incorporate a company to be known as 'The American Salvage Association.' The importance of immediately possessing ourselves of such a valuable name in connection with the syndicates which now seem will certainly be formed [sic] is, I think, obvious. All the other members of the committee were agreeable

xii

to becoming incorporators and I now write to ask if you would not allow me to include your name."

As the following narrative will show, this was not quite the first time that the idea of a separate salvage and survey corporation had been broached. Nor was it quite the name which would ultimately be borne by this book's hero. But, as nearly as such things can be pinpointed, this was the date and place at which the United States Salvage Association was conceived. Its gestation period was to be twice that of a human baby, but, in view of the place it was ultimately to occupy in national affairs, the elephantine pace was perhaps appropriate.

Steamship whistles will furnish much of the background music to the Association's story. But it was a distant locomotive whistle which heralded its inception.

PREMATURE EPILOGUE

THE PROOF OF TWO PUDDINGS

O N February 26, 1960, a thirty-year-old fisherman stood in
Seattle's United States District Court, sentenced to five
years' imprisonment for barratry on the *Cape Douglas,* a fishing
boat of which he had formerly been skipper and part owner.
Barratry, a captain's willful destruction of his own ship, was
long considered in most maritime communities very nearly as
heinous as his murdering a member of his family. Indeed, had
the *Cape Douglas'* master been similarly convicted only 66
years earlier, the judge would have had no option under federal law but to sentence him to death.

What lay behind the case and the conviction was hard
routine professional effort, coupled with alert detective work
on underwriters' behalf, by the United States Salvage Association's Seattle staff, headed by Captain Robert W. Lees, today
its Pacific area principal surveyor.

An eighty-footer, built in 1940 as the *Cutino Bros.,* the
Cape Douglas had been something of a hard luck boat, plagued
with mechanical, operational, and financial troubles and responsible for losses to underwriters of $6,500 in 1958 alone.
She had come to the attention of Lees' office three times during
the same year for valuation surveys precipitated by change of
ownership, addition of new equipment, and change of underwriters. In March she was valued at $65,000; in May, at $80,000,
but in December a requested further increase was denied.

At ten on the evening of December 28, the *Cape Douglas*
was southbound on Puget Sound with no one on board but the
master and a sleeping engineer. A few hours later the pair
landed from a rubber raft at Point Pulley on the Southeast
Seattle shore, reporting that their vessel had foundered rapidly

xv

BACK TO DAYLIGHT

The fishing boat *Cape Douglas* after being raised from Puget Sound.
Williamson photo

after striking some submerged object. What puzzled surveyors and others were the facts that it had taken three times as long as it should to reach the reported point of impact, that an extra-large engineroom had flooded completely in less than two minutes, and that, to come ashore where they did, the survivors must have elected to row several miles against a strong ebb tide, whereas they could without exertion have drifted ashore farther north.

Surveyor Elvin C. Hawley of the Seattle office, today the Association's resident surveyor at Boston, was then making practice flights in a small float plane over Puget Sound, preparing for a CAA checkout. At Lees' suggestion he buzzed the area in question and discovered an oil slick, *five miles south* of the reported point of sinking, at a position whence the life-raft could have drifted practically unaided to the spot where it actually landed, and where the water was far deeper: 106 fathoms. Reportedly no vessel had ever been retrieved from such a depth, but surveyors' and underwriters' suspicions were now so fully aroused that it was determined at least to try to locate the wreck.

Lees learned that a research vessel equipped with newly developed electronic sounding gear of great sophistication was in the area and for hire. Underwriters authorized her use and, with Association personnel in attendance, a series of sweeps were made which disclosed nothing on the bottom at the reported wreck site, but found in the deep water under the oil slick a wooden object approximating the dimensions of the *Cape Douglas,* apparently a vessel on an even keel with the bow pointing southwest. A deep-submergence diving chamber was now sent down and, though the occupant could not see the vessel's name, he fully confirmed all other conclusions drawn from the sounding sweeps and established that the boat on the bottom answered the description of the *Cape Douglas.*

The producers of this nautical mystery drama now faced a final $35,000 question: to raise or not to raise. Fred Devine, the Portland salvage master, stood ready to tackle the unprecedented job, on a "no cure-no pay" basis, for that amount. With an $80,000 total loss claim in the balance—and undoubtedly other such claims in the future if this one were paid—the decision was made to go ahead. Devine thereupon brought in his *Salvage Chief,* a converted LSM which three years later would attempt to aid the stranded *Chickasaw* (see page 157, below), and anchored her over the hulk. Again, Association surveyors were present.

Devine's first plan of attack, to snatch the fisherman off the bottom by grappling, failed as successive superstructure elements crumpled under the strain. Next, with the electronic scanning gear again standing by to give pinpoint precision to his operations, he slipped a lasso of steel wire around the after part of the wreck, hoisted her to 50 fathoms with the *Salvage Chief's* powerful winches, and towed her beneath the surface in a nose-down position to shallow water, where conventional slings could be fitted and the 75-ton weight brought to the surface by a derrick.

As soon as the *Cape Douglas* (for it was unquestionably

she) was drained and capable of being boarded, Captain Lees inspected her with a party which included Coast Guard, FBI, and U.S. Attorney's Office representatives. The signs of barratry were conclusive and damning. All sea valves and bilge suction valves were open and, except for the broken superstructure, nothing else was physically amiss. Once the valves were closed and the boat pumped out, she floated, in Lees' words, "without so much as a teacup of water entering the hull."

Thus, through coldly professional evaluation and pursuit of the clues to waterborne crime, the tragedy of the *Cape Douglas* was brought to a happy ending for all but her hapless ex-master, who was arrested as a crewman on another fishing boat in Alaska less than seven months after his seemingly successful effort to put her where no one would ever find her.

And the Association's office filed its report, closed its case, and went on to other matters.

⚓ ⚓ ⚓

Eight years and a quarter after the *Cape Douglas* touched down on the muddy bottom of Puget Sound, a vessel over five hundred times her size ground to a stop on a rocky outcrop of the British Isles known to seafarers as the Seven Stones. Despite all that men could do, the *Torrey Canyon* stayed and died there, spilling crude oil in quantities never envisioned in any ecologist's wildest nightmare, killing fish, fowl, and marine vegetation, ruining beaches, upsetting local economies, and even jarring the foundations of international amity.

The American Hull Insurance Syndicate was heavily involved as underwriter, and hence the gargantuan casualty was a problem for the United States Salvage Association—in this case the European area office in London, headed by Robert E. Gross.

Within hours a Dutch salvage firm had been retained and was rushing tugs to the area (on one of which the Association's first representative arrived), while simultaneously conducting an airlift of pumps, compressors, and other equipment to the closest field in Cornwall. Use of this equipment, coupled with leakage of oil from punctured tanks, set up an agonizing dilemma: the urgent necessity to refloat the ship versus the explosive hazard resulting from compressed air being forced into partially-empty tanks, with the risk of sparks setting off explosive mixtures of petroleum vapor.

The prime obligation of Association surveyors to their Syndicate principals was to take all possible measures to minimize recognizable potential losses, which meant, in the first instance, prompt refloating of the ship. However, no competent engineer could fail to perceive that refloating efforts already underway carried with them grave danger of explosions which could defeat their own objective and imperil lives. Hence a bridge conference on safety procedures was convened while salvors continued to work in other parts of the vessel. Within minutes, however, this was broken up by the very eventuality it was seeking to avert, a heavy explosion in the stern, closely followed by a second. Lest a "chain reaction" ensue, running the ship's entire length, it was decided to evacuate all hands into one of the tugs standing by.

At first it had seemed that the entire salvage crew was miraculously unscathed, though it had been working throughout the after section of the ship. But, as the tug came alongside, it found the salvage master in the water, where he had been thrown when struck by a piece of wreckage arcing like a projectile over the heads of nearer crewmen to where he was standing, farther from the blast than anyone else aboard except the party in the bridge structure! Though rushed to Penzance, he died of his injuries.

Providentially, no one was inside the stern quarters when the explosions touched off, for in addition to disintegrating the swimming pool (the *Torrey Canyon* was then one of the most luxurious tankers afloat) they literally inflated the inner compartments, driving cabin bulkheads outward, almost to the exterior shell of the after house. When the Association's surveyor later reboarded the ship he found that the engineer's room which he and an English surveyor had shared the evening before had been compressed in width from about twelve feet to a few inches, with all its furniture squeezed between.

Though her tragedy has been told and retold, it has not been widely realized that the *Torrey Canyon* killed a man

The supertanker *Torrey Canyon* as the salvors found her.
United Kingdom Government/Royal Navy photos

before she began killing other creatures. In spite of her proven
deadliness, however, surveyors and salvors stayed at their duties
aboard her, under increasingly trying conditions, until hope of
detaching her from her rocky bed was given up nine days after
the stranding, and attention shifted to desperate efforts to control the consequences of her break-up.

⚓ ⚓ ⚓

The *Cape Douglas* and *Torrey Canyon* cases are a world
apart in terms of the tonnage and insurance values involved;
but each illustrates in its own way the talents and traits of the
men of the United States Salvage Association, and the capabili-
ties and ideals of the organization which these men and others
like them have built over the middle half of the twentieth century. How they did it is the theme of the following chapters.

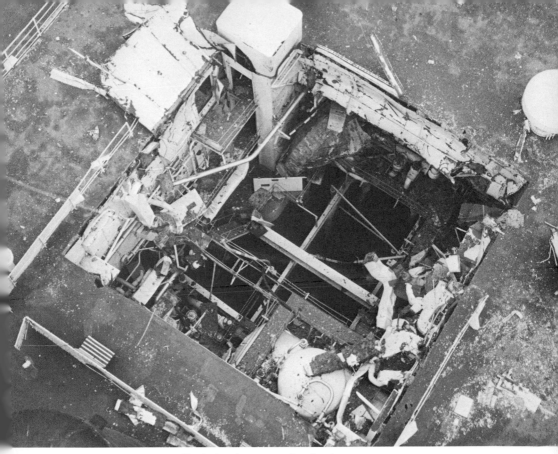

Explosion damage to the after house.

Bombed and broken, showing explosion area directly forward of funnel.

I

THE GENEALOGY OF SALVAGE

THOUGH the intricacies of modern ocean commerce make it hard to believe, there was a long period in history when shipping was, like most other vocations, a one-man venture. The individual who conned and maintained the ship also owned her and, until well into the middle ages, bore all risks of the voyage. Thereafter, by a sort of maritime natural selection, this omnicompetent mariner-merchant evolved and subdivided until by the nineteenth century three interdependent persons stood in his place: the navigator, who depended for his vessel and cargo on the shipowner, who depended for insurance of his risks on the marine underwriter, who depended for technical intelligence as to the risks insured on the marine surveyor. What made this a triangle rather than a four-link chain was that the surveyor was almost invariably a master mariner—not, of course, the one who had run the ship ashore, but an older and presumably wiser professional brother.

With the advent of power-driven metal hulls, the ranks of marine surveyors were swelled by men of engineering and shipbuilding backgrounds, and a new professional technology emerged in what had once been deemed the exclusive preserve of shipmasters who had swallowed the anchor. Today, behind the complexities and confusion of American shipping, essentially the same triangular pattern persists. Its three points are the corporate (often conglomerate) shipowner, the domestic marine insurance market (mainly represented, for hull underwriting purposes, by the American Hull Insurance Syndicate), and the United States Salvage Association, Inc., which observes its fiftieth anniversary in 1971.

Though new as to form and scope when it was incorporated in 1921, the Association was not without antecedents, in this country and abroad. Before glancing backward, however, we should try to define two words we are already using rather freely, "salvage" and "survey." Both are from the Norman French heritage of the English admiralty courts. As verbs, they mean literally "to save" and "to look over carefully"; but, as nouns, both have acquired trade meanings apart from everyday conversational usage—"salvage" in particular.

To most landsmen, exposed only occasionally to shipwreck news on radio or television, it means chiefly if not exclusively the often dramatic emergency operations by which damaged, wrecked, or sunken ships are rescued and delivered to repair facilities where they can be restored to operating condition. To marine underwriters, admiralty lawyers, and marine surveyors, on the other hand, such "salvage" is only one aspect of a much broader abstract concept, and is not necessarily what comes first to mind when the word is used. To them it also means whatever can be preserved or retrieved from a marine loss, whether in terms of cargo, of equipment, or of the ship itself. It can mean, in a certain sense, the cost of effecting the recovery. In the vernacular of the marketplace, then, "salvage" may serve as shorthand for "salvage value," "salvage operation," "salvage award," or simply salvaged property; but the full concept is always in the background. It is in this broad sense (always setting aside cargo salvage) that the word is used in the title "United States Salvage Association."

In the glossary of the Association, which has described itself as "an organization of marine surveyors," the words "survey," "surveyor," and "surveying" also connote something quite different from their meaning to the well-known man in the street. Instead of referring to the measurement of land with level and transit, they concern the equally venerable but little understood art of detailed examination of ships on behalf of hull underwriters, owners, or government agencies. In the literal sense of the Old French term, marine surveyors serve these ships by *looking them over with care*.

⚓ ⚓ ⚓

The underwriter's dependence on the surveyor is ancient and extensive. To take it no farther back than 140 years, one of the first acts of the then recently established Board of Underwriters of New York was to appoint, in all ports and on all coasts commonly visited by American ships, agents whose duty it would be to perform, or to arrange and supervise, surveys of damaged ships and cargo on insurers' behalf. Written authority was given such agents as against all other parties, captains included, to determine when a survey was required. As early as April, 1833, the Board took formal steps "to acquire possession of the funds which have passed into the hands of different parties as the proceeds of wrecked vessels and cargoes insured by and sold for account of the underwriters of this city."

In a day of wooden ships and sparse navigation aids, shipwreck was much likelier to be a terminal affliction than it is today. Understandably, primary emphasis was laid on securing and protecting cargo since, apart from a few stores and deck fittings, cargo was likely to yield the only salvage. Nevertheless, increasing attention was paid to means of protecting and succoring the ship herself. The New York Board's most important mid-nineteenth century employee was its General Agent, a marine surveyor and salvage master who had strategic direction of agency activity at wrecks, and was responsible for the custody and deployment of the Board's own salvage—or, in the terminology of that day, wrecking—equipment. Among distinguished holders of this position between 1840 and 1870 were Captains Henry Holdredge, Russell Sturgis, and Israel J. Merritt.

Despite the early tendency, divergent from present American practice, to lump hull and cargo surveying in the same organizational framework, the major branches of the hull surveyor's function were clearly defined by a century ago. Broadly, they fell—and still do—into three categories: protective or evaluative activities, remedial activities, and general technical and safety activities. The marine surveyor might be called the physician to ships, these three activities corresponding to physical examinations, diagnosis of injury or disease, and medical research in the interest of general health and standardized practice. In the terminology of this book the physical examina-

3

A Nineteenth-Century Salvage Master
Captain Israel J. Merritt
General Agent, The Board of Underwriters of New York

tion is the condition survey; diagnosis and prescription of remedies, the damage survey; while medical research equates to technical studies of repetitive structural and mechanical failures, in contemplation of safer, more dependable ship design.

The rise of industrial specialization after the Civil War could not fail to affect the broad and still loosely defined profession of marine surveying. As has been seen, underwriters expected a wide range of services from their technical officers. Certain of these, it developed, could be rendered most efficiently by corporate bodies exclusively devoted to them. Conspicuous among such spin-offs were the salvage firm and the classification society—the first comprising surveyors whose primary concern was the physical rescue of distressed vessels; the second, surveyors devoted to setting standards and maintaining "quality control" in ship construction. The Board of Underwriters of New

4

York could claim parentage of a great American institution in each area, through its sale of its wrecking facilities to Captain Merritt in 1880, to lay the foundation of the renowned Merritt-Chapman & Scott Corporation (whose salvage facilities were recently acquired by the Murphy Pacific Marine Salvage Company), and its sponsorship in 1862 of the American Shipmasters' Association, now the American Bureau of Shipping, this country's counterpart to Lloyd's Register of Shipping.

Concurrently with the drastic decline in United States ocean shipping during the late nineteenth and early twentieth centuries, insurance of hulls by American underwriters became almost nonexistent. The less depressed state of domestic cargo underwriting resulted in the organizational predominance of cargo over hull surveying. For example, the New York Board, as early as 1871, employed one "Inspector of Vessel Repairs," as against two "Inspectors of Vessels Loading Grain and Other Cargoes," the latter drawing the higher salaries. Hull surveying was necessary, of course, regardless of where insurance was placed; but the fact that the surveyor normally represented a London underwriter seems to have inhibited development of any distinctively American hull-surveying organization.

Meanwhile the major boards of underwriters were virtually converting themselves into cargo-surveying organizations. These included, in the East, the New York Board and the National Board of Marine Underwriters, founded in 1881; in the West, the Board of Marine Underwriters of San Francisco, founded in 1865. In increasing degree, all lost their initial character as insurance trade associations after the formation in 1898 of the American Institute of Marine Underwriters, and became instead technical associations primarily interested in cargo inspection. The New York Board also devoted much attention to salvage arbitration and awards, while the National Board, until the two were merged in 1921, concentrated so intensely on its Inspection Department that for years it planned to reorganize as a "marine salvage and protective association." In fact, in abortive reincorporation proposals of 1899 and 1902 it considered adopting the exact name "United States Salvage Association."

5

At about the start of the first world war, the few American companies still writing hull insurance joined with certain "admitted" foreign competitors in an informal organization under the name American Hull Underwriters' Association. Primarily conceived in the hope (forlorn, as it turned out) of stabilizing rates, its intended functions also included, according to the late Solomon S. Huebner, the appointment of surveyors for ships "about to engage in ocean service." This seeming reference to the nationwide wartime scavenger hunt for any sort of tonnage that might strengthen our almost nonexistent deep-sea merchant marine is all we know about this function of that Association, which became inactive not long after the 1918 Armistice. However, the fact that this organization, rather than either of the eastern boards, was coordinating hull surveys for American underwriters suggests that the typically American principle of separating cargo from hull surveying was already becoming established on the Atlantic seaboard.

On the Pacific, the San Francisco Board still adhered to the older combined practice. It would continue to employ both cargo and hull surveyors—often the same men—down to the 1950's. Then, in the space of a few months, it would divest itself of both activities, combining its cargo inspection division with that of the New York Board to form the National Cargo Bureau, Inc., and giving up its hull surveys to the United States Salvage Association, Inc., which it had already represented for many years.

But this is getting us considerably ahead of our story.

II

SYNDICATE "A,"
THE LAUNCHING PLATFORM

THE incorporation of the United States Salvage Association
was a somewhat deferred incident of the establishment in
1920, with government encouragement, of the American Marine Insurance Syndicates. For an extended account of that
epochal development in American underwriting the reader is
referred to the lately-published history of the American Hull
Insurance Syndicate, *Touching the Adventures and Perils.* . . .
All that is here called for is a summary adequate to explain the
origins of the Salvage Association, and of its predecessor and
"launching platform," Syndicate "A."

The latter and its companion underwriting syndicates,
"B" and "C," were the product of more than two years' negotiation between the United States Shipping Board, both houses
of Congress, and private American marine insurance interests.
This negotiation had in turn been precipitated by the shock
with which the American people and Government discovered
the decayed condition of their merchant marine when the first
world war erupted. In the Shipping Act of 1916, which ordained
construction of an emergency fleet to repair this lack, Congress
recognized that native hull insurance facilities were as depleted
as native shipping capacity, and directed the Shipping Board to
explore means of expanding them.

Nor was the third point of the triangle, marine surveying,
overlooked. The Shipping Board consistently sought such services for its large new fleet, whether self-insured or not. During
the 1919 insurance hearings before the House Committee, Representative George W. Edmonds, the most articulate legislative
advocate of the syndicate plan, referred approvingly to a proposal "that we establish a salvage organization around the

7

world . . . so as to cut down the cost of insurance." And late that same year the Association of Marine Underwriters of the United States, representing virtually the entire domestic marine market, submitted at Edmonds' request a plan whereby the proposed syndicate "will provide the inspection system for such of the [Shipping] Board's steamers as may be entered with the syndicate and also for representation at loss surveys—the syndicate also to advise the Shipping Board as to all loss matters."

Though another half-year was to pass before the Syndicates were formally inaugurated, this proposal, which Edmonds promptly approved, became the official mission of Syndicate "A" as ultimately constituted, with one important addition: inspection and loss-surveying of privately-owned vessels, for a fee. This had not been included in the earliest proposals because at that stage the syndicate scheme was envisaged strictly as a means of insuring Shipping Board hull interests and furnishing requisite survey service on the vessels involved. Participating insurers hoped from the start for a broader arrangement in which *all* American ships would be involved—except for the rather jerry-built fleet of wooden steamers produced under the emergency program, which they steadfastly declined to touch. But not until late February, 1920, was it clear that Congress, too, desired hull insurance facilities available to the entire merchant marine. This settled, the three-syndicate scheme became a matter of course.

To help make it a working reality, Congress passed the Merchant Marine Act of June 5, 1920, Section 29 of which, sponsored by Representative Edmonds, specifically exempted the companies involved in this or any similar combined insurance effort from the operation of the antitrust laws. Such permission to combine was regarded by Congress as essential to the generation of enough underwriting capacity to handle the Shipping Board fleet and to cope with foreign competition.

June 30, 1920, was the date on which the American Marine Insurance Syndicates—and, by ancestry, the United States Salvage Association—came into being. Syndicate "B," which became moribund in a very few years, underwrote government interests in the new fleet which, hopefully, was to be sold to private owners. Syndicate "C" stood ready to insure all steel, privately-owned American ocean vessels (including buyers' equities in Syndicate "B" hulls) . Syndicate "A," with which we are henceforth mainly concerned, requires fuller description.

In the language of the Articles of Agreement subscribed by its member companies, its purposes were "to perform, at cost, Surveying Inspection and Loss services for the United States Shipping Board and United States Shipping Board Emergency Fleet Corporation, in respect to all steel vessels owned by [them] and in respect to all steel vessels sold by [them] on a part payment basis, and to perform similar services in respect to any vessels for any other shipowners and for other marine underwriters upon payment of reasonable charges for such services." As spelled out separately in more detail, it was to render three condition surveys per year on the entire Emergency Fleet (then in the main laid up) and to attend damage surveys on ships in service under government ownership or mortgage.

For its part the Shipping Board promised an initial allocation of $1,000,000, to be drawn on as needed for operating costs, followed by quarterly increments of $250,000. The subscribing companies in their turn guaranteed a fund of $125,000, each contributing in the same percentage as its subscription to underwriting Syndicate "B." Fees for private work would go to abate the Government's outlay.

In short, this earliest incarnation of the Salvage Association was not merely a nonprofit organization but, in effect, a sub-agency of the Government, permitted to do private work for the Government's benefit, not its own. One senses an official estimate that the private surveys wouldn't amount to much, though every little bit would be welcome. If this were indeed the Shipping Board's view, it was happily misguided. Though "outside business" was slow in starting, it was never negligible, and this was fortunate, since a $500,000 payment against the initially promised million was the only outright grant of public funds ever received by Syndicate "A" or its successor.

Because of this primary dedication to government service, membership in Syndicates "A" and "B" (as previously in the Association of Marine Underwriters of the United States, for

9

the same reason) was restricted to companies controlled by United States citizens. Though admitted foreign companies were subscribers to Syndicate "C" from the start, this nationality restriction of Syndicate "A" persisted for many years after the Shipping Board completely withdrew its sponsorship.

The approximate year-and-one-half following June 30, 1920, was a strenuous ground-breaking period for all three syndicates, but especially for Syndicate "A." Technical and clerical staff had to be assembled, office space found, outport operations lined up, and procedural guidelines established. On top of all, it worked out that, in practice though not in the Articles, Syndicate "A" was the organization on which these and similar "housekeeping" responsibilities devolved, for all the syndicates.

That the launching of Syndicate "A" would be the most arduous part of the tripartite program had been foreseen by Benjamin Rush, president of the Insurance Company of North America and of the Association of Marine Underwriters of the United States, as early as February 18, 1920, when he presented the "A" and "B" plans to the Association for approval. Calling it the "bigger proposition" of the two, he said, "It contemplates the organization of a service department for the United States Mercantile Marine . . . not only in the United States but throughout the world. . . . I doubt whether there is capacity throughout the world to do it until we are able to acquire a sufficient number of surveyors and settling agents . . . but we have got to equip ourselves to do it if we are to see that the Mercantile Marine of the United States gets the service to which it is entitled. It is not a money-making proposition for anybody. We will be obliged, all of us, to contribute a heavy tax in our personnel and in our service to get the thing going, but it ought to be done."

It started being done with the election of Rush as chairman of the nine-man Board of Managers which would govern all three syndicates. The other elected board members were Louis F. Burke, Home Insurance Company; Hendon Chubb, Sea Insurance Company (Chubb & Son); Douglas F. Cox, London & Scottish Assurance Corporation (Appleton & Cox);

William R. Hedge, Boston Insurance Company; Edwin C. Jameson, Globe & Rutgers Fire Insurance Company; William H. McGee, St. Paul Fire & Marine Insurance Company (Wm. H. McGee & Co.) ; Walter W. Parsons, Atlantic Mutual Insurance Company; Gomer H. Rees, Continental Insurance Company. Parsons was named vice chairman, Rees secretary. After some delay, an appointive treasurership was filled by W. L. Soleau, from the Emergency Fleet Corporation.

Pivotal salaried appointment, from the standpoint of this history, was that of Charles R. Page, a former Shipping Board commissioner, as manager of Syndicate "A." Later to become president of the Fireman's Fund Insurance Company, with which he had started his career, Page went vigorously to work on the Syndicates' first business day. In the ensuing eighteen months he would be responsible for a major share of the leg-work and key decisions which established all three organizations —and especially Syndicate "A" and the United States Salvage Association—as going concerns.

With the active collaboration of McGee, then serving as voluntary underwriter for the other two syndicates, Page established the central headquarters in New York, first in McGee's own premises at 15 William Street, and by the late summer of 1920 at 44 Beaver Street. Here the Syndicates and Association remained until a 1925 shift to 56 Beaver Street, which was followed in 1933 by a further move to their present address, 99 John Street. A Washington office was also opened, in deference to government wishes, but New York remained the working center.

The most pressing need was to bring together a technical staff and to establish branch offices to cope with the veritable mountain of survey business the Government had waiting. Page combed such sources of professional talent as the Navy, Shipping Board, American Bureau of Shipping, steamship lines, and shipyards, and within a half-year had assembled a body of key men some of whom were to remain with the Salvage Association for three decades.

As chief surveyor, in mid-September, he recruited ship-builder W. C. Foley, previously with Cramp's and Newport

Benjamin Rush, first President of the United States Salvage Association.

News. Foley's interesting sideline was submarines, his prewar career having included four years as supervisor of submarine construction for the Austrian Government and several with the Lake Torpedo Boat Company. It is told of Foley, who was in reasonably comfortable financial circumstances, that he asked the management to reduce his $7,000 salary to $5,000, on grounds that the "job was not worth it." Deputy chief surveyor was J. A. Wilson, a veteran marine engineer. The master mariner side of the house was represented by Captain George S. Bull, who had commanded in sail and served with distinction as chief officer of the Pacific coast express liner *Northern Pacific*.

Under intense pressure to get Syndicate "A" facilities in operation at ports outside New York, Page and Foley toured the Atlantic and Gulf coasts and by the end of the year had established the following offices under the indicated resident surveyors: Baltimore, John C. Mitchell; New Orleans, W. N. Howell; Galveston, John E. Hoover. Five more were added in 1921: Philadelphia, Jay H. Meseroll; Norfolk, James T. Christie; Savannah, Mark H. Winner; Boston, John E. Tull; San Francisco, David C. Young. Agencies were established in other ports, notably Jacksonville, Walter Mucklow, and Seattle, where Captain S. B. Gibbs ably represented the Syndicate and Association until his death in 1928.

A very ambitious program of agency representation in overseas ports was also launched. Early in 1921 Page reported that G. L. Buchanan, Havana representative of the American Bureau of Shipping, would serve as Syndicate "A's" agent. A year later, it could be reported that agents had been appointed at 88 foreign ports, and that representatives were being sought in Germany, the Levant, Africa, Asia, and the East Indies. "We have endeavored . . . to place our interests in the hands of established business houses in the shipping trade, giving preference to American firms or individuals."

That this was no mere paper expansion, the record of survey work performed in the first year and one-half eloquently testifies. Page set November 1, 1920, as the date by which Syndicate "A" "would positively be able to take the business of the Shipping Board at all ports between Boston and Newport News." This deadline was met, with the New York and Baltimore offices open for business, and the Gulf close behind. On December 16 the New York office was reported "complete as far as surveying is concerned" and "in position to send competent men to Boston and Canadian waters, if need be."

Considering that all this organization had to be pulled together on short notice and almost literally out of thin air, the tally of surveys from November 1, 1920, to February 1, 1922, is remarkable. It shows approximately 2,900 condition surveys for the Shipping Board and 2,263 damage surveys for the same client. The domestic grand total for the period was some 6,000 surveys attended. Total Syndicate "A" income from this work was $281,980.49, also impressive for a new venture, though it must be remembered that all prices were still distorted by postwar inflation.

As anticipated, the new organization's weakest showing was in the private business area, with only 786 surveys, for income of $38,356.90. Clearly the subscribing companies of Syndicate "A" were channeling little of their business to it, despite an early-August notice to members "that the syndicates known as 'A,' 'B,' and 'C' have been completed and are now in full force and effect." A more pointed notice to subscribers and brokers, November 4, "that Syndicate 'A' is now equipped to render" surveying service was followed by a December 9 invitation to "all of the loss men from the offices of the subscribing members to come to a meeting at the Syndicate offices" and learn "all about the operations of Syndicate 'A.'" But still private business continued slow, and for years such appeals to members to patronize their own facilities were a regular activity of Syndicate and Association management.

To a degree, the reported volume of Shipping Board work, particularly condition surveys, is misleading, as a result of a classic case of the Government's right hand not knowing what its left was doing. On April 15, 1920, after more than a year's solicitous involvement in planning the syndicates, the Shipping Board quietly entered into a commercial contract for many of the same services which Syndicate "A" was being created to perform. The contractor was the United States Bureau of Survey, an enterprise of two prominent New York marine surveyors and engineers, Frank S. Martin and J. Howland Gardner. It was subsequently stated that certain Board commissioners, either unaware of or unimpressed by the proposed syndicates, had consummated this conflicting agreement without the knowledge of their colleagues or counsel.

The announcement was received with considerable indignation in insurance quarters and on Capitol Hill, where Representative Edmonds was reported ready to demand abrogation by the Board. Cooler counsel ruled in the underwriter camp, however. Besides the obvious political unwisdom of alienating even part of the Government at this juncture, it could not be denied that Martin and Gardner's professional credentials were of the highest, or that they had a working mechanism already in being, in contrast to Syndicate "A's" as yet purely hypothetical organization. One by one, in almost the same terms, Rush, McGee, Hedge, and Chubb advised a worried Thacher not to pursue "a policy of abrogation but rather one of definition and limitation."

In this conciliatory vein, Rush and Chubb on May 6 met with Martin and Gardner and worked out a *modus vivendi*. Spheres of activity were established, with the Board's concurrence, while a paramount position was assured Syndicate "A" through its becoming in effect the Board's intermediary with respect to the specific classes of work assigned the Bureau, mainly condition surveys. These would be reported and compensated through Syndicate "A"—of course "at a price which would give a reasonable profit to the Martin-Gardner group."

Thus what had looked like a disaster proved beneficial, in many respects, for both sides. The Bureau realized at least part of the benefits anticipated from its contract, and the Syndicate was allowed a breathing spell to concentrate on organizing and on damage survey work while gearing to take over the full condition survey task as well. The magnitude of this task is indicated in the figure of 1,189 surveys reported by the Bureau through the Syndicate up to December 30.

By the dawn of 1921 the Shipping Board, weary of this needlessly expensive dual arrangement, exercised its right to terminate the Martin-Gardner contract, notifying Syndicate "A" to prepare to take over all survey work itself. This Page agreed to do by April 1, at which date the Bureau had made a total of 2,298 condition surveys. Efforts had earlier been made to interest Martin and Gardner in merging their operation into the Syndicate, but dropped when Page found their terms "entirely too extravagant." No similar overtures seem to have been made now that Syndicate "A" was more fully organized and manned. However, something of the United States Bureau of Survey survived, through the appointment of two of its men, Christie and Winner, as resident surveyors of the Syndicate's Norfolk and Savannah offices.

III

ENTER THE ASSOCIATION

I N the background of all these early labors of Syndicate "A" lay the idea of a survey and salvage corporation. This idea, as we have seen, substantially antedated the inception of the Syndicates themselves. The leaders of the Association of Marine Underwriters, in their audacious planning for a self-sufficient American hull insurance market, perforce looked to British models, among which was the Salvage Association, London, founded in 1856, incorporated in 1867, and recognized around the world as the indispensable technical auxiliary of the English market. With this example before them, they seem to have felt from the start that the new American insurance facilities would need something more formal in structure than a surveying syndicate.

On February 5, 1920, in his final plans for the first two syndicates, Archibald Thacher explicitly suggested "an American salvage and loss association under federal charter." Though the meeting which adopted the Syndicate "A" and "B" plans thirteen days later tabled a resolution calling for such an association, Thacher was not discouraged. His club-car renewal of the proposition on April 10 was more successful—so much so that from this date the question was no longer whether there would be an incorporated salvage association, but when. This became a matter of priorities.

Obviously much fuller discussion and agreement among the participants would be called for, as well as renewed drafting effort on Thacher's part. There would be no time for this in the next three months—months which included the entire development of "C," largest and longest-lived of the Syndicates. The same period included the passage of the Merchant Marine Act of 1920, the consummation of multiple agreements with the

W. C. FOLEY, Chief Surveyor
Syndicate "A" and United States Salvage Association, 1920-1929

Shipping Board, the jolting setback of the Martin-Gardner imbroglio, the completion of subscriptions, and the staffing and structuring of the threefold organization. The blueprinting of the United States Salvage Association had to wait.

It was not forgotten, however. The Syndicate Board of Managers resolved July 27, "that the aim of Syndicate 'A' should be to develop as soon as practicable an independent organization to take care of maintenance inspection and loss survey service." On September 16, Page and Thacher were "empowered to formulate a plan for utilizing a corporation" to assume Syndicate "A's" functions, and by early November that plan was ready for disclosure to the Shipping Board which, as a primary party at interest, would have to approve any realignment of Syndicate "A" operation.

The early notion of a "federal charter" eventuated in a "dummy" corporation being set up in Washington—apparently for political reasons—but, partly because of residence requirements in the District of Columbia, the main effort was concentrated on incorporation in New York. Thacher's draft certificate of incorporation and by-laws, as well as the basic working agreement between the new association and Syndicate "A" plus a supplementary agreement between the latter and the Shipping Board, received the blessing of the board of managers on February 10 and 17, and of the Syndicate "A" subscribers on the 24th. Filing formalities were completed early in March, and "the first and annual meeting of the subscribers, incorporators, and stockholders of the United States Salvage Association, Inc., was held at 44 Beaver Street," March 31, 1921.

To the legally unsophisticated eye, there was an almost carbon-copy identity between the group which conducted this meeting and that which convened the same day as American Marine Insurance Syndicates "A" and "B." The Association stockholders were the same companies as the Syndicate "A" subscribers. The twelve men comprising the Association board of directors were ten of the Syndicate board of managers plus Page, who was a Syndicate board member *ex officio,* and Lawrence J. Brengle, the Syndicate "B" and "C" underwriter, who would play a leading role in Association affairs for the next fifteen years. The officers, too, were the same—Rush, Parsons, Rees, and Soleau—though the first two bore the titles president and vice president, rather than chairman and vice chairman. Finally, the Certificate of Incorporation made it clear that, in contrast to the Association's broad charter powers today, the mission of the new corporation was to carry on the same work already commenced by Syndicate "A."

Why this "distinction without a difference"? Nowhere do the early documents examined spell out the founders' reason for preferring the corporate form so strongly. A few seem self-evident, however. One is the potential liability attending the survey function. Boarding and inspecting ships, examining marine casualty damage, and in effect certifying to a vessel's state of health (as the Association did in its early years) bore seeds of litigation quite different in variety and complexity from those to which underwriters are normally exposed—litigation in which a corporate person of limited assets would be a much neater, more manageable party than a voluntary syndicate. Probably, too, it was felt that the bookkeeping and financing of the services which the Association was taking over could be most efficiently performed by a corporation. This was to become increasingly true with the withdrawal of the Shipping Board and public funding, an eventuality foreseen by Rush, for one, from the outset. And, finally, there was always the strongly persuasive precedent of London's incorporated Salvage Association.

At all events, the stockholders seem to have been almost unanimous on March 31 that they now possessed the optimum agency for handling the services promised in the 1920 Articles of Agreement. We must say "almost," for, strangely, another half-year was to pass before the Association actually took up Syndicate "A's" day-to-day burdens. The work was already going on, the same people were doing it, the Martin-Gardner cloud had dissolved. What prevented a smooth transition to the new order?

One man alone, it would seem. When the new agreements were approved, it had been done by ballot, with the understanding that the requisite signing by the Shipping Board and member companies would follow at individual convenience. Syndicate "A" could not lay down its burdens, or the Association pick them up, until all signatures had been affixed. Within a few weeks this had been accomplished, except for one signer— Samuel Bird, Jr., whose office represented three domestic insurance companies, the Aetna, the Franklin Fire, and the Springfield Fire and Marine. Came summer and, despite Page's protest at a July 7 meeting that "the failure of these companies to sign the agreement is embarrassing because it must be signed by all parties to be effective, and it is impossible to proceed with the development of the United States Salvage Association until that agreement has been executed," Bird (say the minutes) "was not prepared to sign at the present time, nor was he prepared to give his reason for not signing."

Though the rest of the board finally broke the deadlock in late summer by authorizing Page and Hedge to go directly to the companies, bypassing Bird, the latter seems never to have relaxed or explained his fixed opposition to the new organization. The summer before, he had had strong disagreements with most of his fellow board members which had caused him to withdraw his companies from Syndicate "C" before it was two months old, and which may have colored his attitude a year later. At all events, he remained firmly consistent, and, though outmaneuvered, resigned from the Association board of directors eight days before it ultimately became operational.

That long-deferred event fell on October 18, 1921, when the Association took over Syndicate "A's" staff, agents, offices, and service commitments, financed by a $50,000 advance from the funds which the Syndicate continued to administer as intermediary between the Shipping Board and the Association. Henceforth the original "service syndicate" would confine itself to a fiscal and liaison role.

Another and more important resignation coincided with the Association's activation: that of Syndicate "A's" manager and its own, Charles R. Page. Like Bird, his recent adversary, Page gave no written reason for cutting short, as of December 31, what was to have been a three-year appointment. The minutes mention an oral explanation, but do not elaborate. A sufficient *post hoc* explanation was his almost immediate appointment as Atlantic Marine Department manager of his old company, the Fireman's Fund, in which capacity he assumed the seat on the board vacated by Bird, as well as the chairmanship of a newly created Management Committee of Syndicate "A" and the Association.

Behind this change of employment, however, lies the probable further reason that Page was finding his managerial role less attractive than sixteen months earlier. He was a man of action and had plunged ambitiously into the creation and building up of an American survey organization. Now, with the 1921 shipping slump, "Slow Ahead" had become the order of the day. As early as mid-June he had reported to the board of managers that business conditions were so bad he had "really nothing to report." He used almost identical language in reporting to the meeting which accepted his resignation. It may be going too far to read disillusion into these evidences, but certainly some of the zest had gone out of the game, and seemed likely to stay out for several years.

IV

EXIT THE SHIPPING BOARD

A LL things considered, the maiden departure of the United
States Salvage Association was taken under less than
auspicious circumstances. The economic weather was foul, and
plainly deteriorating. The chief customer, the Government,
was already showing some reluctance to pay the freight. And
the navigator was packing his gear to go ashore.

The third problem had to be dealt with first. Fortunately,
there was ample talent already on board to relieve Page. On
the latter's motion, Brengle was persuaded to add the managership of Syndicate "A" and the Association to his underwriting
responsibilities. John H. Trowbridge, who had joined the
Syndicates in their first weeks, was named assistant manager,
a title whose duties he would discharge with great credit for
nine years.

A further year-end change was the resignation of Gomer
Rees as secretary of the Syndicates and Association, and his
replacement by Norman S. Adams, the assistant secretary, who
would hold office for over 22 years.

As to the business climate Page's comments, already cited,
by no means painted too dark a picture. The bottom had
dropped out of the shipping boom into which the Syndicates
had been born. With ships going into layup all over the world,
the prospects of rapid, profitable sale of the Shipping Board's
fleet, and the Association's related plans for worldwide servicing
of that fleet, suddenly contracted. Over three months before
the Association takeover, Page informed the Shipping Board
that because of these conditions "the Syndicate had made little
or none of that development abroad which was anticipated,"
foreclosing for years the possibility of direct branch offices in
foreign ports. By November, 1921, he was convinced that the

organization was overextended even at home. With the active Shipping Board fleet down to about 400 vessels (as against 870 nine months earlier), several offices established "when our business anticipated at least a thousand Government-owned vessels in operation" already looked like "losing propositions." These misgivings were borne out in December, with the closing of the Philadelphia office and the halving of the Savannah staff.

The swift deflation of the balloon cut tonnage values in half. It had a similar effect on repair costs, because of the decrease in operational vessels and the consequent cutthroat competition for repair work. Foley's report of January 19, 1922, that such costs were "about 50% less" than a year before was by no means bad news for underwriters, if taken out of context. Unhappily, the full context included the fact that income to the underwriters' own survey organization had also been drastically deflated. Syndicate "A" and the Association had performed 4,393 domestic surveys in 1921, the latter, 4,358 in 1922 (a year in which its foreign agencies reported an additional 266 surveys). Yet income from this work was only $188,363 in 1922, as against the $281,980 of 1921.

The Association could not await final returns before mov-

Idle Shipping Board vessels laid up off Staten Island, a scene repeated at many anchorages around the coast in the twenties.   *Author's collection*

ing to cope with this clearly impending loss. On March 9, 1922, it announced a cut in surveying staff from 21 to 15, even though the "volume of work now handled is higher than any previous months, except April and June." Such retrenchment was to be the story of the next three years, as Shipping Board surveys shrank from 3,286 to 1,604 and total domestic work, even with a steady increase in private surveys, from 4,358 to 3,451. By May 21, 1925, Brengle and Foley still felt "that a reduction in the number of surveyors at New York was advisable" in view of diminishing government work. The upshot included Wilson's departure and the abolition on June 15 of his office of deputy chief surveyor.

The decade from 1921 to 1931 was marked by two opposing trends: the gradual retirement of the Shipping Board from its commitments of 1920 and the slow but steady upbuilding of United States Salvage Association services to private industry. On the balance ultimately struck by these trends depended the success of the Association, if not indeed its survival. Consider first the stages by which the Government made its exit.

The planning of Syndicate "A," so far as the Shipping Board and its Emergency Fleet Corporation were concerned, had been premised on the sale of some 1,400 ships built under the mandate of the Shipping Act of 1916. By the time the Association replaced Syndicate "A," almost 1,000 of these remained in layup with no prospect of imminent disposal. Since the obligation to perform condition surveys applied to operational ships only, there was an immediate decline in this area of anticipated service. For five years starting with 1921, the annual totals of condition surveys performed were: 1,344, 1,044, 945, 876, 703. Damage surveys, covering losses to ships in which the Government had equity, were more numerous and declined more slowly: 2,263, 2,242, 2,130, 1,699, 901.

These trends, coupled with an opinion of the General Accounting Office that such an outright monetary grant as had been provided under the Syndicate "A" agreement was possibly illegal, seem to have given the Shipping Board second thoughts. Though, as we have seen, only half of the million dollars initially pledged was ever paid, and though the Syndicate voluntarily waived every $250,000 quarterly payment on grounds that the half-million plus its own subscriber-contributed revolving fund fully covered its operating costs, the Board was already hinting by late 1921 that it might demand the return of $200,000 of its first payment. The Syndicate/Association considered it unfair for the Government to avoid its contract because of unforeseen conditions which affected both sides adversely; but clearly two of its first orders of business must be to seek mutually acceptable adjustments of the agreement and to develop new spheres of service to the Government.

For legalistic reasons, the Shipping Board refused in May, 1922, to entertain the customary waiver of payment, saying "it will not be obligatory [for the Government] to make any further payments," and so set the stage for six months' negotiation to amend the Syndicate "A" agreement, negotiations spurred by its service on September 26 of the prescribed 90-day notice of termination. Arrival at new terms, effective January 1, 1923, caused the notice to be withdrawn. These terms, foreseeably, excused the Board from any future payments, establishing instead a $125,000 revolving fund on which the Association would draw as necessary and which the Board agreed to maintain so long as Congressional appropriations permitted. Brengle and Thacher believed that this fund, with the subscribers' own fund in the same amount, "together with . . . monthly accounts, should be sufficient to finance Syndicate 'A' under present shipping conditions."

It will be seen that the revised contract was still with Syndicate "A," not the United States Salvage Association. A direct Government agreement with the latter had been suggested, but the Board negotiator had advised against it, "as the name and nature of Syndicate 'A' are so well known in Washington."

Probably the most significant extension of service to the Shipping Board in these years was a program of special condition survey work undertaken at the request of both the Board's Cargo Rating Committee and the Cargo Underwriters' Conference Committee. Its general object was to rectify alleged lax maintenance and slipshod operation of many government-owned, privately operated vessels, a condition which had tended to cloud the status for insurance purposes of the entire Shipping Board Fleet. As stated by Brengle in May, 1922, the program's objects were " (1) to ascertain that these ships are not being overloaded, (2) that the reasonable requirements of our periodical condition surveys are carried out, (3) to keep in touch with the personnel of the Board vessels—in other words, to keep a general check on those ships." A year later he reported excellent cooperation by operators eager to secure "liner" or "approved steamer" ratings, a "most hearty response from the Shipping Board," and the establishment of a system for notifying underwriters "of those ships meeting with our approval." Some of the accepted recommendations, he said, "have called for structural alterations of an extensive character, . . . to place the vessels in the front rank as cargo carriers."

The Association also apprised the Board that underwriters blamed the unsatisfactory situation in part on "unnecessary transfer by Shipping Board operators of Masters and Chief Engineers from one vessel to another." As a result the Board warned all operators against such changes, "whereby ships have suffered in operating efficiency," and directed "that no Master or Chief Engineer who has actually been to sea in the vessel to which he is attached is to be replaced until the matter has been referred to this office."

Washington's respect for Association rulings is further illustrated by three cases in which unsafe operating practices were effectively opposed during this period. Late in 1923, on Surveyor Tull's protest that the steamer *St. Anthony* was one foot two inches overloaded, the Board forbade her sailing from Boston until she had been lightened. A few weeks later, when the Board steamer *Cuprum* left Seattle for Vancouver partly laden, drawing 31 feet aft and 10 forward, the strong protest of Captain Gibbs, the Association's Seattle agent, elicited assurances that "proper action" would be taken for the future. In August, 1925, surveyors found the turbine reduction gears of the privately-operated Board steamer *West Gotomska* so badly worn that they refused a certificate of seaworthiness for her scheduled voyage to the Baltic. Even though she had previously been cleared by the Shipping Board and one other agency, she was thereupon "removed from the list of approved steamers," with notice to the Board and the cargo underwriters.

The Board also responded constructively to Association criticism of its passenger fleet, notably the war-designed "502" and "535" classes of passenger-cargo vessels, so-called from their length. On November 16, 1922, Page reported that the "502's" had "developed a very important—not a serious, but an important—weakness in the after lower holds," and added that the Association had succeeded "in imposing conditions on the Shipping Board that these vessels shall carry no cargoes in these holds until these repairs have been properly made." In December it was reported that they were being made, as a "result of constant effort on our part with the Shipping Board for the last six months." Soon afterward, the "535's," starting with the North Atlantic liner *President Roosevelt*, developed cargo-damaging leaks in their No. 1 and 2 holds. After months of pressure by Foley, it was finally announced in October, 1924, that the Board was giving this vessel and her sisters "extra stiffening . . . which will overcome the trouble and make the ships better in every way."

Also evidencing the prevailing atmosphere of reasonable give-and-take was the Association's willingness to give serious consideration in July, 1924, to the Board's request that it open an office in Mobile, and the Board's acquiescence in dropping the idea five months later, in view of "present conditions."

But, however friendly the atmosphere, the Board's scope of activity was relentlessly narrowing, and with it the need of Association service as originally envisioned. Ship sales, which had amounted to 271 before the slump, resumed but on a diminishing basis: 127 vessels being disposed of in 1925; 88 in 1928. The stress was now on disposing of "lines," the berth services on "essential trade routes" which the Board had established under the 1920 Act, and operated through agents pending sale to private operators. As each sale was consummated, the Board's need of Association surveys, and of its own worldwide network of offices, declined.

In the fall of 1925 the Government exerted pressure to

A Shipping Board type "535." The passenger ship *President Harding,* sister to the *President Roosevelt* mentioned in the text.   Author's collection

amend the agreement further in its own interest. Resultant concessions relieved it of the obligation to "enter" with the Syndicates all vessels it sold, though it agreed to use its good offices to induce the private purchasers to enter them. In partial compensation, it enlarged its obligation to enter government-owned operational steel ships so as to include tugs.

After a decrease in both categories of government surveys in 1926, the trend was momentarily reversed in 1927 with an increase in condition surveys from 637 to 685 as a "result of a renewed effort on the part of the Board to maintain its ships in condition to merit the complete confidence of underwriters," and a three-year increase in damage surveys from 867 to 933, apparently generated by a new Board policy of relying on the Association "to protect its interests on damaged steamers in which the Shipping Board Insurance Fund is interested as Underwriter."

But this was the last gasp. For 1929, condition surveys

dropped 90% to a mere 64, with a total of 997 of both kinds. In 1930, with the Depression in full swing, the total dropped to 625, and the Shipping Board decided to call it a day. A notification of intent to terminate the agreement at the end of the year was demurred to by the Association on grounds of its having built up a "considerable organization involving the expense of establishing a number of exclusive offices in the principal United States ports and a wide network of about one hundred and fifty agencies abroad" and "in view of the existing widespread business depression." In response, the Board made an ultimate concession: while reducing the revolving fund to $75,000, it consented to extend the agreement for six months, and to institute a "Lump Sum Plan" under which the Association would perform two condition surveys a year "on somewhat over one hundred vessels."

The Depression continued to deepen, however, and the Shipping Board allowed all agreements to lapse on June 30, 1931. These included the Lump Sum condition surveys, which had produced a small terminal bulge in total government statistics to 662. From now on, the United States Salvage Association was entirely on its own, though with assurance that the Board's Merchant Fleet Corporation "maintains its interest in the progress and success" of the Association. Not until the fall of 1935, however, was a "final agreement" signed, "thus closing on our books the old account with the Shipping Board."

The *Leviathan* at sea in September, 1929, three months before developing her hull crack (see p. 40). The tall structure at the stern is the "Adams Air Mail Pickup" apparatus used experimentally for transfer of mail to and from aircraft in flight that month. *UPI photo*

V

"IN THE MERCHANT CATEGORY"

THE growth of private work, initially treated as a sideline by the Government (and even, it would appear, by some of the Syndicate "A" subscribers) was to be the most distinctive feature of the Association's first decade and, in a real sense, its anchor to windward. Had the early predominance of government work continued (an emphasis which caused Page on July 7, 1921, to view Syndicate "A's" activities as "largely supplementary to those of a government bureau" and to describe its successor on December 15 as having evolved into "a survey bureau instead of on the broader lines of a salvage association") the organization would have had no choice in 1931 but to fade from the scene with the Shipping Board.

But to anyone who troubled to read the signs it was clear from the start that the Association was not headed in this direction. Indeed, the Board's withdrawal, when it came, seems to have been welcomed by the Association staff with a sense of challenging release—whatever the reactions of underwriters. Retired surveyor Andrew S. Varni recalls that it "gave us all satisfaction . . . made us feel on our own. It freed us from the 'Navy' atmosphere and put us in the 'Merchant' category, which we all liked, and where we belonged."

After 1921's weak showing, Brengle reported a record total of 97 private jobs during January, 1922. By the annual meeting, March 9, Foley could say, "Our private survey work . . . is now 130% more than it was a year ago." At the 1923 meeting, non-government business was "running over 100 surveys per month," and three years later the monthly average had risen to 136 in New York alone.

By 1930, the last full year of the Shipping Board agreement, this slow welling up of private business had virtually turned the annual percentage ratios upside down. In 1921 private surveys had been only 17.9% of total surveys attended, accounting for only 13.6% of income generated. In 1930 they amounted to 85.1% of Association work, by number; 69.8% in dollar value. Since no profit was involved from any of this, private survey income being applied to offset the Shipping Board's financial contribution, the Association was not only fortifying its own standing as a viable commercial entity, but substantially weakening the hardship plea on which the Government essentially based its ultimate abrogation of the agreement. Some idea of the extent to which the public financial burden was thus eased may be read in the fact that, between 1922 (when postwar inflation had passed) and 1930, total survey income, from governmental and private sources, rose by 33.8%, even though this included a drop of 43.9% in Shipping Board survey income.

This headway had been made in the face of active competition for commercial survey work. First, there were the private surveyors, many of whom had continuing arrangements to handle certain owners' or underwriters' business. Organizations like Frank Martin's did not go out of business merely because the Government decided to abide by its original exclusive commitments to the Syndicates. Moreover, longstanding company relationships were not readily set aside. In August, 1921, the Syndicate with "regret" had to advise one member, the Automobile Insurance Company, that that firm's own surveyor could not be associated with Syndicate "A" surveyors on damage surveys. The problem was still serious enough in 1927 to evoke a protest from the Insurance Company of North America that, for a survey of a dredge in which it and "probably fifteen" other companies were interested, it alone had called on the United States Salvage Association (of which most if not all were stockholders) and so had to foot the entire bill.

There was also significant if scattered competitive overlap with the field representatives of the American Bureau of Shipping. Though the Bureau's president and vice president, Stevenson Taylor and E. P. Bertholf, had testified in the 1919 congressional hearings that it did not engage in such loss surveying as was contemplated for Syndicate "A" (Bertholf in particular saying such work was "a bit beyond the function of a classification society") there was no question that, well into the thirties, many Bureau field men unofficially doubled in brass as loss surveyors, notably in Great Lakes and foreign ports.

Finally, there was the United States Salvage Association's well-entrenched prototype, the Salvage Association, London. After a half-century's near-monopoly of ocean and Great Lakes hull insurance by the British market, that Association's representatives were strategically distributed around the globe. Diplomatic overtures by Brengle and others established reasonably cordial relations by the fall of 1923, when Sir Joseph Lowry, the London Association's chairman, on a visit to New York and San Francisco, stated "that with the cooperation of both Associations much might be accomplished"; but later in the decade the American organization's entry into the Great Lakes would be retarded, in part, by London's strong position there, while it would be many years before economic conditions permitted effective competition in overseas ports.

From the start, the underwriting syndicates—especially "C"—were, as distinct from their individual subscribers, the foremost private users of Association facilities. As early as April, 1921, Syndicates "A" and "C," in separate meetings, studied arrangements "whereby . . . surveyors of Syndicate 'A' would be used exclusively, instead of the old method existing for some time before the Syndicates were in operation." Up to December 15, such arrangements had resulted in "B" and "C" paying "A" "197 bills for surveys and expenses, aggregating $12,106.22." Thereafter, the annual reports, especially of "C," testify to their growing reliance on their own survey organization. For example, in 1927 Brengle, as chief underwriter, notes that the "Association has continued to be of material benefit to us" and commends the "expert nautical knowledge which is made readily available through the surveying personnel of the Association." In 1930 he says "We are indebted to the Association . . . for their help and advice in matters of serious loss."

Further support toward filling the private side of the ledger came from several smaller syndicates created in the mid-twenties to deal with hull interests not insurable in Syndicate "C." The Tug Reinsurance Agreement (later the Tugboat Underwriting Syndicate) gave its business to the Association from its inception in 1925. A dramatic jump in private surveys the next year from 1,847 to 3,461 was, according to the management, "due very largely to our arrangement with the Tug Reinsurance Agreement." In 1929 the Great Lakes Underwriting Syndicate similarly requested the Association to represent it, a development which in due course added some 1,500 private lake surveys per year to the books.

Regular service to foreign shipping in American waters was also inaugurated during this period, including a 1925 agreement that "Association surveyors at Savannah, New Orleans, and Galveston should be employed whenever possible" to represent Norwegian underwriters in damage surveys on ships of that flag.

The gradual swing of private organizations to dependence on the Association was directly related to its visible achievements in serving the Government and the Syndicates, and to its growing stature in the fields of marine technology and safety. Its best selling point throughout was a proven ability to spot inflated repair estimates and get them adjusted.

Contrary to widespread practice in many ports, it followed a consistent policy of calling for competitive bids. When Syndicate "A" was only six months old, Page reported finding a range of $113,821-70,225 in six bids on the damaged *Cornucopia*. On two other vessels, the Syndicate had been able to cut down repair bids from $13,640 to $5,000 and from $5,250 to $1,500. A year later the Association trimmed the repair price on the *Arizonan* from $4,900 to $3,250, and in 1924 a surveyor's ingenuity permitted engine repairs to the *Miller County* without removal of parts to a shop, at a saving of $3,000.

These economies were applauded somewhat less loudly by repair firms than by underwriters and shipowners. On January 18, 1923, in fact, the New Orleans surveyor reported a local repairer's complaint that he might "have to go out of business, and that the Salvage Association would be responsible for it, by

Down-east night liner *City of Rockland* on the Kennebec River ledge which ended her career, 1923.
Mariners Museum photo, courtesy Mr. John L. Lochhead

SIDEWHEELERS IN EXTREMIS (see p. 39)

Hudson River Day Line flagship *Washington Irving* on the bottom of New York's North River, 1926.
Herald-Tribune photo, courtesy Mr. Donald C. Ringwald

our policy of calling bids wherever possible and refusing to agree to their lump sum proposals."

⚓   ⚓   ⚓

The United States Salvage Association and marine safety causes were closely identified from the start. Long before the *St. Anthony* and *Cuprum* incidents, a Syndicate meeting of January 13, 1921, ordered "that definite information be collected on the overloading of tankers, and the owners notified of the unseaworthiness of the same." Establishment of loadline standards became a lasting concern, and in 1928 the organization's future president Samuel D. McComb, of the Marine Office of America, was named to the committee which advised Secretary of Commerce Herbert Hoover in shaping federal loadline legislation enacted the following year.

McComb also served in 1928 on the industry committee to help develop the United States position for the Safety of Life at Sea meetings in London which led to international adoption of the Convention on Safety of Life at Sea, 1929.

Promulgation in 1922 of the first National Fire Protection Association rules for "freeing oil tanks of vapors before repairs are made on tank vessels" met with enthusiastic support from the organization, which has steadily insisted on such gas-freeing to this day. Its underwriter members authorized Brengle to insert, "in all cases possible," a policy warranty of compliance with the NFPA regulations.

The Association naturally took an interest in salvage vessels and their sound maintenance and deployment. It consistently refrained, however, from ownership of such equipment. Thus in 1922 it "welcomed" a proposal by Furness interests that a salvage tug be stationed at St. John's, Newfoundland, but said it "would not be justified in investing any part of the Association's funds." It gave the same answer in 1923 to a proposal of Frank B. Hall & Company, brokers, that it help finance the maintenance of the tug *Central American* at Tampico. However, its direct contact with such vessels and their operators gave it one more field of usefulness, as indicated in the 1924 annual report: "Another service which we are now able to offer our subscribers is information regarding the salvage equipment available at all the principal foreign ports."

An activity of public value transcending its benefit to marine underwriters was a "trouble-shooting" program in the raw boom port of Miami where, during 1925 and 1926, heavy traffic and a disastrous hurricane made shipping and wharf operations congested and hazardous in the extreme. Captain Bull was sent on two fact-finding and correctional trips, doing work "of great value," and "getting before the proper authorities an ordinance dealing with preventative measures as to fire and the proper handling of vessels and cargoes at that port." A permanent Miami agency was also established in charge of Charles A. Auld, who would serve the Association in southern and Great Lakes ports for the next 26 years.

Other safety activities which tended to build prestige were Foley's advocacy in 1923 of a law requiring ships to employ radio direction-finders "in the same manner as the installation of the radio wireless," Association cooperation with other groups in opposing a hazardous drawbridge proposed for the Mississippi River in 1925, and its recommendation in 1927 of a New York fireboat with chemical apparatus capable of extinguishing fires in cargo holds without flooding.

The Miami agency was followed in 1927 by similar representation at Tampa, while in the West Gulf Houston's growing importance was signalized by the assignment of Guy A. Myers as resident surveyor there. Myers, who would remain in the Association's employ until he retired in 1954, worked under William Freeman, in charge at Galveston since 1924, and took over the Texas area when the latter moved to New Orleans in 1929.

One further extension of Association scope was heralded by Brengle's announcement on November 15, 1923, "that he had been approached by Mr. May, Chairman of the Committee on Averages and Arbitration of The Board of Underwriters of New York, with regard to the examination by the Salvage Association of general average adjustments," and that he had accepted the invitation as "extending the usefulness and value of the organization to underwriters."

Such examination might be considered a function more of underwriters than of salvage men—and, in point of fact, the actual work was always performed by the managers of the Syndicate "C" Loss Department. However, it was officially treated throughout as an Association activity. Annual reports from 1924 to 1951 list the number of general average statements reported to the New York Board committee by "our Adjusting Department." While ultimately dropped as an incongruous pursuit for such an organization, there appears no doubt that its nominal sponsorship contributed more than a modicum of prestige in the early years when every bit of available prestige was needed.

VI

DAMSELS IN DISTRESS

WHILE the United States Salvage Association was not created to engage in the sort of ship salvaging popularly
associated with the ocean-roving salvage tug, or with such organizations as Merritt-Chapman & Scott, Foundation Maritime,
Wijsmuller, Bugsier, and L. Smit—in short, the kind of ship
rescue for which salvage awards are made—its surveyors have
always been actively-involved "bystanders" in such operations,
safeguarding the interests of their principals and frequently
acting as advisory participants. Page was authorized, in Syndicate "A's" first summer, to employ a salvage officer; but never
did so, as he explained a year later, first because he could not
find the right man, and second because of the curtailment in
planned service functions.

It does not appear that this particular job title was ever
conferred on any Association employee; but many of its surveyors, from the outset, were fully qualified salvage masters,
and frequently acted in that capacity. The raising of sunken
vessels and the refloating of stranded ones were matters in
which they were fully as well versed as in the examination of
damage or the evaluation of physical condition. And, since
negligent or incompetent procedures in these operations could
greatly increase owners' and underwriters' costs, surveyors'
judgment was heavily relied on in this class of work.

Before it had been operating two months, the Association
was involved in several salvage cases, assisting in the raising
of the new United States submarine S-48, which had sunk on
trials off Bridgeport, Connecticut, and in the refloating of a
drydock from Squibnocket Beach, Martha's Vineyard. Early
in 1922, Captain Bull showed himself a competent salvage
master when he was rushed to South America to oversee the

In December, 1921, while running trials for her builders, the Lake Torpedo Boat Co., the new submarine S 48 sank in Long Island Sound in 60 feet of water. Ejected by torpedo tube, a volunteer from her desperate crew found that, in going down, the boat had hung on Penfield Reef, with her bow and an escape hatch above water.

Courtesy Submarine Force Library and Museum (first two pictures)

THE FIRST ASSOCIATION SALVAGE CASE

Her crew safe, S 48 moves shoreward in the slings of the mighty *Monarch* and a sister derrick.

S 48 under way in later years.
Courtesy Our Navy

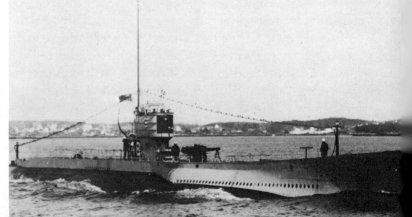

refloating of the steamer *Garfield,* stranded near Puerto Colombia, a job which won high praise from his Syndicate principals.

In each ensuing year, lists of major salvage cases attended were published in the Association's annual report. Though selective, these suggest a steady rise in the number and gravity of casualties attended. As against seven for 1921-2, 33 were listed for 1926-7. Association surveyors were called in on several major collisions involving vessels of the then-flourishing coastwise lines: the Morgan liner *El Sol,* which sank in an affray with the *Sac City* at New York in 1927; the Clyde-Mallory liner *Algonquin,* which sank the Furness Bermuda liner *Fort Victoria* near Ambrose Lightship in 1929; and the Merchants & Miners' *Fairfax,* which collided with the tanker *Pinthis* in Massachusetts Bay in 1930 and was herself swept by fire before the oil carrier sank.

This was still the era of big, luxurious sidewheel steamboats in the coastal and inland passenger trades. Association surveyors stood by two of these in what eventually proved their last extremities. One, the 275-foot *City of Rockland,* was successfully refloated and towed to Boston from a rocky island on which she had stranded in the Kennebec River, September 2, 1923. The other, the 400-foot, three-funneled *Washington Irving,* flagship of the Hudson River Day Line, was raised from the bottom just off her New York pier, where she had sunk June 1, 1926, in collision with an oil barge. Both steamers were, however, adjudged constructive total losses (in that the cost of repairs would exceed their insured values) and neither ever turned a wheel again.

Among successful tanker salvage operations supervised by Association personnel were the refloatings of the *Frank H. Buck* (1924) and the *Tamiahua* (1930) from the California coast—the first near Point Pinos, the second not far outside the Golden Gate. The *Tamiahua* case was reportedly the first major instance in which the Association departed from its competitive bid rule. Though San Francisco was a high-priced repair port, the vessel was "too badly hurt" to be safely or economically moved elsewhere.

By the closing months of the decade, such work had attained impressive financial proportions. In March, 1929, it was stated that "during the year we attended and negotiated salvage operations on marine property having a total insured value of approximately $7,675,000 . . . at United States ports. If we take into account the salvage matters in which our foreign agents participated, the above figure would be greatly increased."

Before the end of that year, the Association would be confronted with a repair job dwarfing any that had gone before. The victim was the *Leviathan,* largest American passenger liner: her damage, two hull cracks sustained in heavy North Atlantic weather, running vertically for three decks, through double and treble plating. The massive job, quite beyond the capacity of most yards, was called "unique in the amount of interior work that has to be done." On the first round, the lowest responsive bid obtained was $528,000. But again the Association, vindicating underwriters' hopes, was able to negotiate a cost reduction to $415,000; though in all probability even that marked the largest partial loss in Hull Syndicate history to that date. Whether the big ship's few remaining years of generally unsuccessful operation justified this outlay is open to question.

The turn of the decade brought casualties requiring Association attendance to four American passenger ships outside the continental United States. In 1930 the Los Angeles Steamship Company's *City of Honolulu* burned at sea, for a constructive total loss. The next year brought far-flung strandings of three "535's": the Munson Line's *Western World* on the Brazilian coast, and the Dollar Line's *President Cleveland* and *President Lincoln,* in China and the Canal Zone, respectively. Despite setbacks, a worldwide United States Salvage Association presence was at last functioning as its founders had envisioned.

But not all (or even most) salvage cases attended were ships large enough to command headlines. The day-in-day-out availability of the Association's ship doctors to make "house calls" and effect cures on humbler craft probably did more than anything else to earn the organization widespread recognition as a reliable and necessary element of the maritime community.

The Clyde Mallory liner *Algonquin* (above) displays her bruised and twisted stem after 1929 collision in which the Furness Bermuda liner *Fort Victoria* (below) went down. *UPI photos*

As one example of such grass-roots activity, and the sort of improvisation it often entailed, Charles Auld recalls the case of a heavy wooden derrick barge planted by a hurricane on a swampy island near Charleston, South Carolina. Costs of dredging a channel to her resting-place became prohibitive when the Government ordered that any such channel be filled afterwards. The island was too soft to permit use of rollers. Finally, at Association suggestion, a crew of men threw up a thirty-inch mud dyke running from the water's edge completely around the barge and back to the water's edge, the space between the two ends being closed by a similar dyke or dam. A dredge then floated the barge by pumping the dyked area full of water and, by pulling on wires, gave it sufficient momentum to break through the dam and ride unharmed into deep water, on its own freshet!

VII

THE GATEWOOD INTERLUDE
AND THE DEPRESSION

THE year 1929, which culminated in the *Leviathan* case, marked, if not a coming of age, a clear-cut "end of the beginning" for the United States Salvage Association. Its survey offices were established on the Atlantic from Boston to Miami, on the Gulf from Tampa to Galveston, and, somewhat less independently, on the Pacific from San Pedro to Seattle. Private surveys by these offices had increased more than 400% since 1921, by number; almost 350% by income.

In 1928 overseas agencies reported 83 cases handled, twenty of them in the Shanghai area. Though broad areas of weakness still existed, the organization was now so well established that the increasingly probable withdrawal of government support no longer posed a mortal threat. The time seemed ripe for new departures.

On February 21, 1929, Brengle, now vice president as well as manager, recommended that someone else take over the latter function, "because the growth of the Association and the Syndicates was such . . . that the welfare of both organizations might suffer in the future if conducted under a common managership." This recommendation led to the appointment on October 15 of Captain Richard D. Gatewood. Brengle simultaneously resigned his managership, though he continued as vice president.

Gatewood had held his captaincy in the Construction Corps of the United States Navy, from which he was newly retired at the age of 47. An alumnus of the Naval Academy (1903) and of graduate work at the Massachusetts Institute of Technology (1906) he was known as a brilliant engineer, having published nine papers and discussions in the Proceedings of the Society

43

of Naval Architects and Marine Engineers between 1916 and 1929. Since the war he had headed the Shipping Board's Maintenance and Repair Department, hence had worked closely with the Association on matters pertaining to Board vessels. He had directed the Board's "dieselization" program with its own ships (the first significant American effort to introduce internal combustion to ocean shipping) and had coordinated the less successful experiments in burning pulverized coal under steamship boilers, experiments for which the steamer *Mercer* served as guinea pig.

In short, the Association had in Richard Gatewood its first chief executive who was not an underwriter but a highly qualified marine technologist. He came to office at a time of ostensible prosperity for both it and the nation, imbued with broad plans for expanding and strengthening the organization and with the will to carry them out. As if to give him greater freedom of action, two of his more energetic predecessors followed Brengle's lead and left the field at this time. On September 5, Charles Page, first manager of Syndicate "A" and since 1922 chairman of the Association's Management Committee, resigned to return to his company's home office in San Francisco. December 19 brought the resignation from the board of directors of Benjamin Rush, principal founder and the Association's first president.

Gatewood plunged at once into inspection, evaluation, and planning. Within a month he had visited all exclusive offices on the Atlantic and Gulf coasts except Savannah, reporting himself pleased with what he found, apart from one or two "round pegs in square holes." Apparently classed among the latter was Foley, whom he considered insufficiently forceful, and replaced as chief surveyor with a former Shipping Board colleague, John A. McKeown. Captain Bull was made deputy chief surveyor at the same time, and several key field men were replaced by surveyors with whom Gatewood had worked previously. The "Navy" manner in which this shakeup was conducted irked some of the existing staff, and Gatewood himself admitted years later that his choice of McKeown over Bull had been a bad mistake. On the whole, however, his personnel choices stood the test of time, notably that of Charles Mallynn at New Orleans (later Galveston) and that of John Rohde at New York "as a specialist in wood work . . . which will relieve Captain Bull, who . . . is too valuable a man for the general run of such work."

On November 21, 1929, the new manager made the first of a number of reports in depth on the organization and his ideas for its future growth. He outlined the personnel actions taken and his efforts to establish "cordial relations with as many representatives of the brokers and underwriters as I could, also with allied offices—the American Bureau, Salvage Association London, and the Shipping Board." Looking to the future, he recognized the need for an expansion into the Great Lakes area and said that, with the directors' approval, he planned "to make immediate survey" of that district, followed by inspection trips to the west coast and Europe.

He concluded his report on a familiar theme, the need of greater stockholder support if the Association were to realize its potential. "My travels around do not indicate that the Underwriters have used the facilities of the Salvage Association to the fullest extent. . . . Surveyors outside our organization are doing the work in too many cases. The more you can do to use the Salvage Association the more it will be to everybody's great advantage. It will help sharpen the instrument and keep it up to its work."

To cope with anticipated increases in volume, Gatewood also announced a reorganization of the southern offices into a South Atlantic and a Gulf District, respectively, under Auld and Freeman as principal surveyors. He would shortly establish a similar format in the Great Lakes area, and seems to have contemplated the same treatment of the Pacific Coast and Europe. Extension to the Mississippi River system in 1930 was even indicated, following up a policy announcement of March 21, 1929, that "inspection of damage repairs to inland marine craft" was to be undertaken.

No one who knows the Association's later history can well escape the impression that the breakout from its early parochial limitations which finally transpired in the fifties could have happened under Gatewood in the thirties but for one of the minor ironies of history: just eight days after his first full-dress report, the Stock Market collapsed and the Depression began. Thereafter no amount of long-range planning and reorganization could stem the precipitate downward plunge of all business, shipping included.

There was no defeatism about the new management, however. Gatewood pressed ahead with his plans, with his fact-finding tours, and with intensified efforts to build up volume in existing offices. He made two swings around the lakes, touching every major port from Duluth to Montreal, in December, 1929, and the summer of 1930, visited the west coast at the end of winter, 1930, and inspected most major European agencies late that spring. Though the expense of these trips was criticized, in a time of falling revenue, it is hard to see how else the diplomatic pressure essential to break into long-established preserves of competing organizations could have been effectively applied.

The simple fact was that receipts from surveys, like all other commercial income, were being inexorably eroded. This was partly obscured by the last-gasp bulge in Shipping Board income already cited—a 9% increase in 1930. No one, however, was in a better position than Gatewood to realize how imminent was the withdrawal of Shipping Board funding. Early in his term of office he suggested that henceforth the Board be regarded simply as a major client, to be billed like any other. Meanwhile he worked, and hoped, for sufficient income to keep the Association's head above water until times improved and the new organizational arrangements could take effect.

Month by month, the stubborn effort to ignore the indicators continued. In May, 1931, Gatewood said, "The outlook . . . is somewhat brighter now than it has been for months," but in July he had to concede that May surveys "had fallen off 10% as compared with May, 1930." In September, "total surveys for the first seven months of . . . 1931 were 311 less (about 13%) than for the same period in 1930." In terms of income, receipts for the six months following government withdrawal were almost 15% below 1930, on an annual basis, and still falling.

There was only one possible end. With Shipping Board financial support withdrawn as of June 30, expansion had to be sacrificed to survival, indefinitely. On November 2, 1931, Gatewood resigned, blaming the "exceedingly depressed condition of the shipping industry" and admitting "that the resultant reduced revenue does not warrant a continuation of the present burden of executive overhead charges." McKeown and several other pre-1929 colleagues left with him.

Thus the Gatewood interlude came to an end. It would be twenty years before the Association attempted another major break with its circumscribed past. But there were permanent gains from this brief period of semi-independent operation. Gatewood's foremost achievement was unquestionably the establishment of a Great Lakes District, to be more fully discussed below. He also roughed out the pattern on which, as we shall see, European and Pacific Coast operations were finally to be set up. Anticipating the technical studies of a later day, he urged "detailed, analytical study of damages, to arrive at definite conclusions as to cause." He left a strong cadre of key men in charge who would see the Association through the Depression and the war years. But he correctly described the bleakness of the immediate outlook when he wrote a correspondent on November 14, 1931, his last day of duty, that "the Board of Directors has indicated an unwillingness to go on with the overhead involved in the present executive control and at least until there are some signs of a real increase in business they want to return to the position of two years ago before I came with the organization." If anything, the Association went back beyond "the position of two years ago," and stayed there for some time.

⚓   ⚓   ⚓

Except that the economic environment was even drearier, the United States Salvage Association found its position in 1932 very similar to that of 1922. Its survey volume was dropping rapidly, both numerically and in dollars earned. Annual income

47

Charles R. Page, 1920-1921
Courtesy Fireman's Fund Insurance Co.

Lawrence J. Brengle, 1922-1929, 1932-1935
Courtesy Mrs. Thomas S. Gates

Captain Richard D. Gatewood, 1930-1931

Michael F. McAlinden, 1936-1941

was running below $200,000 for the first time since 1926. It would fall to $175,339 by 1935, and would average only $186,-800 for 1932-1940, inclusive, as against $207,600 for 1922-1930.

A personal parallel was that, with Gatewood's resignation, as with Page's ten years earlier, it devolved on Brengle to take command of the laboring vessel and somehow steer her clear of the shoals. Still a vice president, he now resumed his old duties as manager also. His assistant was now Michael F. Mc-Alinden, John Trowbridge having been relieved of that office early in 1931 to devote full time to new duties as assistant underwriter of the reorganized Tugboat Underwriting Syndicate. Trowbridge, whom Gatewood describes as "earnest and conscientious," died quite suddenly less than six months after leaving the Association. Eulogizing him at the 1932 annual meeting, Brengle said, "Great credit is due to him for the progress made by the Association during his period of office."

McAlinden, his successor, had come to the Association shortly before the Gatewood regime, and would remain in its service for over a quarter-century. One contemporary who worked closely with him describes him as small, mild, and usually overworked; another as "pleasant, good-natured, somewhat breezy." Though self-effacing, easily overshadowed by more aggressive colleagues, and neither engineer nor surveyor, he had a manifest knack for keeping the office wheels turning and ably discharging duties which lacked appeal for others. The records make it clear that he shared with Brengle and Bull virtually the entire burden of keeping the Association afloat during the worst of the Depression.

When Gatewood left, stringent retrenchment became the order of the day. It was ruled that neither he nor those who had resigned with him should be replaced, in the hope of mitigating economic pressures on remaining employees. By mid-December, 1931, Brengle had rejected the managership application of Charles Skentelbury, formerly of the Shipping Board's London office, and two years later, when the Board proposed as a candidate its outgoing Merchant Fleet Corporation president, Captain Elmer E. Crowley, he still refused, saying the Association could not "increase expenses under existing conditions." Instead he performed the duties of manager himself, without compensation beyond his salary as underwriter for the Syndicates, a fact which the directors acknowledged December 21, 1933, by voting him "a Christmas gratuity of $1,000."

Outside New York, the steady decline in shipping and survey business had already forced the closing of the Baltimore office. John Mitchell, who had been resident surveyor until replaced in 1929 by a Gatewood designee, was now named Association agent at that port, an appointment he would hold for almost two decades. As the Gulf situation worsened, the offices at New Orleans and Houston were similarly discontinued, their incumbent surveyors, Freeman and Mallynn, becoming agents instead. Finally, in 1935, the Savannah office was dropped, surveyor Auld being transferred to Norfolk, from which he would continue to supervise his former territory. Thus, by the latter thirties, the United States Salvage Association had only three permanent offices on the seaboard: Boston, New York, and Norfolk.

These cutbacks, a 10% salary reduction, and other measures gradually overcame a deficit which amounted on January 1, 1933, to $38,194. Syndicate "C," which had heretofore shared office and staff costs on a *pro rata* basis, also helped by agreeing for the present to a flat fee of $6,000 per year, less than half what the Association had been paying. Though shipping conditions remained depressed for many months more, the financial horizon slowly brightened from now on. At the start of 1934 the deficit stood at $19,988; a year later, at only $4,910, and by mid-1935 the red ink bottle could be put away. Meanwhile it had become possible, in July, 1934, to refund to each subscriber which had withdrawn from Syndicate "A" its share of that syndicate's "Assessment Fund," with 6% interest from date of withdrawal. On April 18, 1935, Brengle was given discretionary authority to restore the salary cut, and by the end of that year the Association was able to pay Syndicate "C" $12,500, as "a more equitable share" of annual service costs.

Thus, under Brengle's indefatigable leadership, the United States Salvage Association emerged from the second, and by far the graver, crisis of its first fifteen years. He had received devoted assistance, on the New York front, from McAlinden, Bull, and Ernest W. Schuler, treasurer since Soleau resigned in 1923. Schuler's unrelenting economies earned him an in-house reputation for stinginess, though this was coupled with reluctant admiration. But Brengle was the man primarily responsible for the victory. Sadly, he did not even survive to report it at the 1936 annual meeting, for his sudden and tragic death occurred on February 21 of that year.

The Association was left in charge of his lieutenants, under the broad policy direction of Henry H. Reed of the Insurance Company of North America and Frederick B. McBride of the Fireman's Fund, president and vice president by virtue of their corresponding Syndicate posts. McBride became president in 1937, with William D. Winter of the Atlantic Mutual as vice president and McAlinden as acting manager. Their united efforts, however, could not fill the gap left by Brengle. With business picking up and war looming, the conviction grew that it was time Syndicate and Association had a permanent, appointive chief executive. This was achieved through a contract of employment with William Bradford Harwood (previously Brengle's assistant underwriter from 1920 to 1925), under which, in April, 1938, he was "elected" chairman of the American Marine Insurance Syndicates and president of the United States Salvage Association. At the same election, McAlinden was confirmed as manager. Both were to hold office through the war and for some years thereafter, McAlinden being redesignated executive secretary in 1941.

But, before following up these matters, it is necessary to double back and trace three major geographical extensions which Gatewood had initiated.

VIII

TO THE INLAND SEAS

W HEN Page and Foley were evolving Syndicate "A's" branch office structure they made no provision for the Great Lakes area, partly because the Shipping Board had no fleet interests there, partly because Syndicate "C's" original Articles of Agreement expressly barred the writing of lake risks. The interests of underwriters, British and American, in the Great Lakes fleets were primarily represented, for salvage purposes, by London's Salvage Association, with regional headquarters in Cleveland, long presided over by R. Parry-Jones. Popular and highly respected in both insurance and vessel-owning circles, Parry-Jones relied for surveys not only on his own representatives but also on numerous private surveyors and the local representatives of the American Bureau of Shipping. The Great Lakes Protective Association, an organization of shipowners, with some insurance functions for its members' benefit, also entrusted its work to him.

Brengle felt it unfortunate from the start that American underwriters had no access to an American survey organization on the lakes. On September 17, 1925, having heard that Parry-Jones, who was in advanced years, was planning to retire, he seized the opportunity to recommend that the Syndicates look into extending both their underwriting and their survey activities to the Great Lakes. This first move toward fresh water was brought up short a few weeks later when London chairman Sir Joseph Lowry scotched the rumor of Parry-Jones' retirement at a conference with Brengle in New York.

The matter remained in abeyance until February 7, 1929, when the newly-established Great Lakes Underwriting Syndicate, which shared quarters and staff with Syndicate "C" and included many of its subscribers, voted "that the Salvage Association be requested to extend its operations to the Great Lakes." Two weeks later this invitation was formally accepted, with Brengle "authorized to establish an office in that district."

Matters moved slowly, but from now on they moved. In July Brengle reported having tried without success to recruit C. H. Lincoln, an American Bureau representative, to open an Association office on the lakes. Here things stood until November, when it devolved on Gatewood to find the man who should head the new office.

He found him during his first inspection tour of the Gulf, in Guy A. Myers, the resident surveyor at Galveston. In the words of Carolyn V. McClaskey, Myers' secretary for almost a quarter-century at Cleveland, Gatewood at once "decided that Guy Myers had the essential qualities and abilities to launch— and 'make work'—the Association's . . . Great Lakes enterprise." A native of Charlevoix, Michigan, he had come of age in the enginerooms of "upper lakers." Miss McClaskey, now in the Miami office, describes him as "genial, friendly, . . . gregarious," with a vocabulary "salty, decisive and copiously sprinkled with profanity." James C. Sherman, who succeeded him, says he was "gruff, blunt, and dynamic, with a mind like a steel trap," but remembers, too, his liking for people, his "million stories," and "the laughter in those bright, piercing eyes as he told them."

Above all, Myers had a broad knowledge of lake operations, lake operators, and lake ways. He "spoke the language," a vital qualification in a region always acutely conscious of its marine individuality.

Back from the Gulf, Gatewood lost no time in obtaining official approval of his choice of Myers and his plan for three new exclusive offices, in Cleveland, Buffalo, and Chicago. By the day after Thanksgiving he was in Cleveland on a diplomatic mission to develop friendly, cooperative relations with Parry-Jones and with H. N. Herriman, American Bureau vice president on the lakes. He also sought rapport with individual shipping leaders, including J. S. Ashley, president of the Great Lakes Protective Association. The record suggests that he waged a highly successful public relations campaign, stressing the As-

The French liner *Normandie* arriving in New York on her maiden voyage,
June 5, 1935 (see p. 74). Author's photo

sociation's emphasis on serving those interests which had requested its representation (primarily the Lake Syndicate), and
keyed more to collaboration than to competition.

Myers continued this "missionary" program after his arrival in Cleveland March 15, 1930, as principal surveyor of the
Great Lakes district, to open an office practically adjoining
Parry-Jones' in the Rockefeller Building. This edifice was headquarters for a large segment of the Great Lakes marine community, and Miss McClaskey recalls that almost every morning,
that first year, Myers would "go visiting" around the offices,
rapidly winning friends. Nevertheless, suspicions and even
jealousies persisted in some quarters, and for many months
Myers' energetic efforts had to be actively backed by quiet
diplomacy on the part of Brengle and Gatewood, in New York
and in the field.

A Buffalo office was opened in April, with William T.
Smith as resident surveyor. Opening of a Chicago office was

deferred, however, until business volume warranted the outlay. Instead, arrangements were made for representation, on a fee basis, by the American Bureau's highly respected surveyor there, Alexander Hynd.

With commercial salt-water business dwindling under depression conditions (down 36% in number of surveys, 29% in dollars, between 1930 and 1932), Myers and Gatewood hoped the newly-launched operation would redress the balance. At first, it looked as if this might be achieved: during the first three and one-half years, overall survey volume held about level numerically. But the financial balance sheet told a truer and sadder story.

What was needed, and actively sought, was access to all categories of lake business in which American underwriters were interested—though, even had this been promptly attained, we can now see that it would not have been enough. For Great Lakes shipping was being even harder hit than ocean, as witness Gatewood's reports during the bitter mid-months of 1931 that the Association's overall deficit was almost entirely chargeable to its lake business.

Attainment of such access was painfully slow, hinging on the fleshing-out of a still skeletal organization largely confined to Lake Erie, on enough good public relations and performance to dispel local propensities to view the Association as an interloper, and—most important—on efforts at the head-office level to have Association services written into American policies, preferably as a requirement, not an option.

All this took time, tact, and travel. Myers was constantly on the move, and Gatewood joined him for a July inspection of the enlarged Welland Canal and a September visit to upper lake ports, continuing alone to Montreal (which the Association has since treated as part of its Great Lakes district, with local representation by Hayes, Stuart & Company). During the summer, continuing problems of communication between Myers and Parry-Jones were finally resolved, with agreement on full interchange of information in cases involving American insurers.

The major breakthrough which assured the future of the

lake venture did not come, however, until February, 1931, when the Great Lakes Underwriting Syndicate decided to specify in its policies that the United States Salvage Association perform surveys and supervise damage repairs on its assureds' vessels, and that it also supervise winter mooring of such vessels at the major layup port of Buffalo. While this decision did not immediately, as Gatewood prophesied, "change the results from red to black figures," it justified his boast that it "completely changes our status on the Lakes from now on."

The winter mooring job, heretofore performed by the American Bureau of Shipping (though its officials "were free to admit that this work was not normally work for a classification society"), had been desired by the Association in 1930. Opposition on the part of the Great Lakes Protective Association to such an innovation had, however, been strong enough to delay the change for a year. To date, Bureau personnel had also handled the inspection of grain cargoes, one of the lakes' two most important waterborne commodities. Shortly after the Lake Syndicate action, the powerful Grain Classification Committee, representing most interests involved in this trade, moved to transfer the inspection function to the Association, to be performed in Cleveland and Buffalo by its own staff, in other ports, by Bureau representatives under its "general supervision."

While these changes were endorsed by Bureau headquarters in New York, they provoked enough grumbling along the lakefront to evoke assurances from Gatewood of efforts to do the work "at no increased cost to owners, and without unduly hurting the revenue of the American Bureau," plus confidential instructions to Myers "to visit all the American Bureau offices . . . and . . . the Toronto office of the British Corporation and Lloyd's, and have a face-to-face talk with the men in charge . . . before the season begins." Meanwhile the Association drew up and distributed its standard instructions for damage surveys and grain inspections which, as amended, remain the basic rules of procedure on the lakes today.

All this did not mean that "prosperity was just around the corner," for the Association any more than for the rest of the country; but it did guarantee the ultimate success of the Great

Lakes operation. By 1934 Myers, who had been assisted from the start by W. G. Atherholt, a veteran of the New York Office, was authorized to enlist a young trainee in addition. Two years later, prestige and prospects were dramatically enhanced when the Great Lakes Protective Association, which had hitherto left selection of surveying entities to its members' option, announced that henceforth their certificates would "require that notification of damage and survey be made to the United States Salvage Association, . . . who will in the future represent that Association in all salvage cases." This designation, and an appointment to represent both American and British underwriters on the upper lakers of Canada Steamship Lines, signalized the full coming of age of the United States Salvage Association on the lakes.

These developments, plus an uneven but sustained increase in volume from the low of the mid-thirties, revived plans for a Chicago office. To implement them another veteran surveyor, Charles Auld, was brought west from Norfolk at the start of navigation in 1937. After a season in Cleveland "learning the territory," he opened an office in Chicago's Board of Trade Building May 1, 1938. In its first two full seasons (1939-1940), McAlinden reported as manager that this office performed 493 surveys for a billing of $19,000, "fully justifying our expectations that the branch would be self-sustaining." By 1941, when J. A. Fuhrman relieved Auld of what he calls his "temporary duty," the new upper lakes office was thus making a significant contribution to the Association's Great Lakes income, which increased 27% in the four years before Pearl Harbor.

IX

TO THE GOLDEN GATE
AND THE GOLDEN HORN

GATEWOOD's strategic plans for the Association also envisioned stronger, more direct operations in two broad territories where it was then represented only by agents: the Pacific seaboard and Europe. Both programs ended inconclusively upon his resignation and, what with depression and war, it would be over twenty years before either area had the exclusive office toward which his efforts trended. Enough foundations were laid, however, to require brief review here of the Association's position in these two regions after its first decade.

Initially, we have seen, San Francisco was one of the ports where Syndicate "A" felt bound by its Shipping Board commitments to establish its own office. This it did April 1, 1921, naming David C. Young as resident surveyor. Young's territory was the California coast. For the Northwest, Page considered a separate office needlessly extravagant, and instead obtained permission from the Board of Marine Underwriters of San Francisco to utilize their Seattle agent, Captain S. B. Gibbs. Gibbs' Syndicate responsibilities, covering the Oregon, Washington, and British Columbia coasts, also took effect April 1. At Syndicate "A's" annual meeting it was further noted that "this arrangement will . . . bring to the command of the Syndicate a highly specialized knowledge of the difficult conditions obtaining in Alaska."

When the United States Salvage Association inherited these western facilities six months later, San Francisco already looked like a poor investment. This was confirmed when year-end returns for 1922 showed only 179 surveys performed by Young's office, as against 1,706 by New York, 806 by New Orleans, and an average of 301 by the other five Atlantic and Gulf offices.

58

The tanker *Tamiahua* ashore off Pescadero, California, in 1930 (see p. 39). Expensively refloated and repaired, she survived to become, as the *W. D. Anderson*, one of the first million-dollar U-boat losses of 1942.   *Author's collection*

The chief problem was the San Francisco Board which, as we know, had its own corps of surveyors, both hull and cargo, and as a matter of course looked after most private business of its underwriter members, even though these were largely western branches of companies which also subscribed to the Syndicates and owned the stock of the Association. The inevitable result was that Young was largely restricted to Shipping Board business, which was proving less plentiful than expected.

Upon Brengle's glum report, June 15, 1922, "that the [San Francisco] Board . . . has not yet seen fit to cooperate in any way with the United States Salvage Association," McComb volunteered as a committee of one to go west and seek solutions on the spot. Reporting back a month later, he said most offices, though Syndicate members, seemed to feel a primary duty to the Board, and to look askance at Young as "principally a machinery surveyor." He advised, farsightedly, that, "if these two offices could be merged into one without any loss of identity on the part of either, . . . it would be very beneficial."

Over two years would elapse, however, before this practical resolution of the impasse was achieved. To Brengle's suggestion that they employ Young in a dual capacity, the San Francisco Board replied in August, 1922, that they already had two salaried surveyors and needed no more. Seeming to hark back to shipping and surveying practice of an earlier day, they also assigned the rather surprising reason "that during the past twelve months they have had no steel vessels to survey," giving Brengle the impression "that they look on Mr. Young as an engineer (steel) surveyor, which they are not particularly concerned about."

But Young's professional reputation in other Coast circles was already rising at a rate the Board could not long ignore. During that same summer of 1922 the Shipping Board was advised by its district director, F. W. Relyea, that Young was "very valuable" to them and "should be continued with the U.S. Salvage Association." On the private side he was highly praised for having "saved the owners and underwriters a great many thousands of dollars" by his handling at Los Angeles of the *Wm. A. McKenney's* damage in her collision with the *Ginyo Maru*. In the upshot, the San Francisco Board had a change of heart and wrote Brengle in September, 1924, seeking "to obtain Mr. Young as its Chief Surveyor." By November 20 this had been carried into effect along the lines already suggested by McComb, with Young employed by the Board but simultaneously under contract as agent of the Association.

Basically, this was to be the West Coast working arrangement for thirty years. It was a generally satisfactory arrangement, especially when strong personalities like Young and Gibbs were involved. Its chief weaknesses seem to have been in the subsidiary ports, staffed by old-line Board surveyors, where the adage about two masters often applied. It was to tying up these loose ends, and to strengthening the Association's hand in an area too unwieldy to be efficiently handled by one man in San Francisco, that Gatewood addressed himself on his first (and, as it turned out, last) inspection tour early in 1930. With his accustomed energy and assurance, he set about meeting as many as possible of the underwriting, shipping, and shipyard leaders throughout the area, under the tutelage of Charles Page, now established in the Fireman's Fund home office.

With an eye primarily and properly to Association needs, Gatewood became convinced that Young was badly overworked and that certain of the resident port surveyors left much to be desired—though he was highly impressed with A. H. Bryant, who had succeeded Gibbs at Seattle, and with Captain Charles Clarkson at Vancouver, British Columbia. In person and by subsequent correspondence, he importuned President Livingston of the San Francisco Board to secure a deputy chief surveyor for Young and replacements for several port surveyors, notably at Portland, Oregon, and Wilmington, California. He even nominated his own candidates, chiefly former Navy and Shipping Board colleagues.

These proposals, which Page gently suggested had been over-impetuous, were considered by the Board and rejected, on grounds of expense. But Gatewood's mission was by no means a failure. Its most important and lasting result was agreement on the first clear-cut and comprehensive set of ground rules for the Board-Association collaboration. As reported to the directors on March 20, 1930, these were:

(1) That the Board . . . is the Agent of the . . . Association and will perform the necessary work for it with its corps of surveyors, with Mr. David Young as Chief Surveyor for all Pacific Coast ports, all important decisions to receive his personal approval.

(2) That the Surveyors of the Board performing . . . Association work will continue to be appointed by it and paid by it, but that appointments . . . will be subject to the prior approval of the Manager of the . . . Association.

(3) That the identity of the . . . Association will be preserved in every possible way.

(4) That the utmost consideration and courtesy will be used at all times in the conduct of the business of the . . . Association and every effort made to make all concerned feel that they have been dealt with in a spirit of eminent fairness and courtesy.

(5) That because of the necessity for prompt action, the home office of the . . . Association will continue to deal directly with and from Seattle on matters under its jurisdiction.

(6) That in matters involving the policy of the . . . Association, the Manager thereof may deal directly with those employees of the Board . . . engaged in performing work for the . . . Association, advising the Board or its Chief Surveyor of the circumstances of such dealings.

Under these principles, at least until the almost simultaneous deaths of Young and Bryant in February, 1938, the United States Salvage Association probably had the strongest standing on the Coast that it could have in the absence of actual branch offices. So great was its reliance on Young that, when general economic conditions forced the Board to cut his salary by $2,000 in December, 1934, the Association made up the difference, and continued to do so until his death.

By then the New York office was in the throes of reorganization and, although McAlinden was sent west to assist in finding Young's replacement, the major initiative for maintaining a joint survey system on the Pacific seems to have passed to the

The "535"-class transpacific liner *President Madison* lies capsized against the Seattle dock where she had been under repair, with side plating removed, 1933 (see p. 67). *Courtesy Mr. Frank O. Braynard*

EMBARRASSED PRESIDENT

San Francisco Board, for the duration. A dozen years would go by before active attention was again directed to establishing the independent facilities first envisioned in 1920.

⚓ ⚓ ⚓

In his first formal report to the directors, November 21, 1929, Gatewood promised to look into the status of Association representation abroad, particularly in Europe. By this date the agency structure covered approximately 150 foreign ports, as against 88 in 1922. Europe and the Mediterranean had the largest number of any single geographical area—over 40—largely because the Shipping Board's foreign operations, now steadily diminishing, had always been most heavily concentrated there. As already noted, overseas business had from the start run so far short of anticipations that minimal attention had seemed called for. The annual total of 266 foreign surveys in 1922 (194 of them for the Government) had never been approached since, and the surprising 126 private surveys reported for 1926 was about three times the annual average for the period. The year before Gatewood took office saw only 83 cases "dealt with abroad"—both public and private.

The new manager believed something must be done to improve this situation, and he saw in the Shipping Board's impending withdrawal from the foreign scene an opportunity for major enlargement of Association activity and prestige. Adding urgency were the misgivings already voiced by Brengle over reports that a commercial surveying operation was being planned to take over the servicing of Shipping Board tonnage in Europe. These reports apparently stemmed from the well-aired hopes of Captain P. C. Grening, the Board's director for Europe, to perpetuate his organization on a private footing after the Government withdrew. Such an arrangement, though of course contravening the Board's still-extant agreement with Syndicate "A," might nevertheless prevail unless the Association acted to strengthen its overseas presence.

In March, 1930, Gatewood announced that as a first step he would visit "the principal agencies in Europe, as they have never been inspected and there has been very little contact except by letter." He did so in April and May, calling on representatives in England, France, Italy, Germany, Denmark, Holland, and Belgium, and concluding that, while some agent-appointed surveyors needed replacement, the agencies were mostly "in the hands of outstanding and reliable people." During the year he also devoted much effort to enlarging worldwide representation, adding "some 30 new agencies" and raising the grand total of foreign ports covered by 1931 above 180.

On his tour he met one man who would come to play a leading role in the Association's overseas affairs. George R. Alden, engineering specialist and former U.S. Navy warrant officer, had served for years on Grening's staff, latterly in Hamburg. Faced with imminent termination of this job, he was planning to set up a private surveying office in that port, hopefully with a contract to represent the Association. Though impressed with his abilities, Gatewood could not in fairness break off the longstanding and satisfactory Hamburg agency of Henry Schmidt, nor was he ever able, with income plummeting, to place Alden on a proposed retainer as a sort of roving surveyor for North Europe. He did, however, put him in touch with McComb, then Association president, and with Captain Charles A. McAllister, president of the American Bureau of Shipping, which led to his receiving a certain amount of P. & I. work for American underwriters and an appointment as Bureau surveyor at Hamburg.

By these efforts on Alden's behalf, seemingly unproductive at the time, Gatewood left one more lasting mark on the organization. Fourteen months after his resignation, his protege was appointed by Brengle, on McComb's recommendation, as the Association's General European Surveyor and Salvage Officer. Times were still hard enough in January, 1933, so that no retainer went with the title—Alden was to be paid for his services when and as rendered. But a cordial 21-year working relationship was thus launched which the Association would later find invaluable.

All European agents were instructed to report "casualties involving large amounts" to Alden, but compliance was so uneven that in December Brengle appointed Alden General European Agent, in direct charge of the whole European agency network. Though still on a fee basis, and never a direct employee, he was henceforth the Association's main link with its most important overseas interests, exercising authority comparable to that of the principal surveyor of a district.

Until 1936 he continued to operate from Hamburg. But the Shipping Board (now in process of being supplanted by the U.S. Maritime Commission) had been urging the superior merits of London as a control center, and McAlinden and the directors took advantage of Alden's presence in New York that summer to make arrangements for moving their European headquarters across the North Sea. Ominous developments in Germany no doubt entered into the decision, as well.

Significant both of improved economic conditions and of Alden's mounting value to the organization was the fact that his revised agency agreement for the first time involved financial guarantees, "sufficient to cover his estimated expense of maintaining such headquarters." Under its terms Alden opened a London office November 1, 1936, which, in addition to its continental scope, supplanted the existing local agency of W. K. Webster & Company. It was specified that this "would not be the Association's office" and that Alden was "free to do other work," but from now on—and especially during the war years— it constituted the organization's recognized transatlantic operating base.

One provision of the agreement was that Alden "import from this country a young man whom he could train up, so that he would have an American there to carry on should a necessity arise." This led to his employing Edward F. Ganly, who would be prominent in foreign and domestic operations down to the sixties. Alden did not quite meet expenses out of fees earned in his first year; but Association Vice President William Winter, who inspected his establishment in the summer of 1937, "considered it remarkable that starting a new venture he came as near as he did to making both ends meet" and reported himself convinced that they were "very fortunate in having Mr. Alden to represent the Association abroad." Rising returns in ensuing months would vindicate Winter's optimism, until the events of September, 1939, dramatically altered the situation.

Merchants & Miners liner *Fairfax* in wartime transport service twelve years after her collision with the *Pinthis* (see p. 39)   *Steamship Historical Society of America*

X

FROM THE *MORRO CASTLE*
TO THE NEUTRALITY ACT

For the Association as a whole, the middle and late thirties were a severe testing time. With staff and facilities still at austerity levels, it was called on to complete its own recovery while keeping step with the nation's, to survive the body blow of Brengle's death, and to cope with a succession of damage and disaster cases exceeding anything in its prior experience.

For the nine years preceding Pearl Harbor, the annual reports describe 128 salvage cases as "outstanding." Even allowing for the fact that this is a selection, and for the random distribution of accidents, these lists reflect a significant geographic imbalance in calls for attendance of major casualties. One-third relate to the Atlantic seaboard; another third to the Great Lakes. The remaining third divide evenly into 21 Pacific-Gulf-Inland River cases and 21 cases outside the continental United States and Canada. These statistics strongly suggest the unprofitability of the West Coast arrangement and leave little doubt that the decision to establish Great Lakes offices was fully justifying itself by the mid-thirties. In these same years Lakes income averaged 32% of total income.

The half-dozen cases which space permits us to single out do some violence to these statistical generalizations, in that only three occurred within the continental limits, and one of these was on the Pacific Coast. The nine-year period was ushered in by two grave mishaps of 1933, half a world apart. In the eastern Mediterranean, the new European Surveyorship was put to the test when the war-built freighter *Exarch* of the Export Steamship Corporation (forerunner of today's American Export Isbrandtsen Lines) drove ashore on Cyprus. At Seattle, the American Mail Line's "535" passenger liner *President*

Blackened skeleton of the
Havana cruise liner
Morro Castle stranded on
Asbury Park beach in
September, 1934.
Author's photo

Dining saloon.

Promenade deck.

Boat deck (note bolts which held wooden deck planking)

Madison suddenly capsized while lying alongside a repair dock. The prompt personal attendance of George Alden at Cyprus, and of David Young at Seattle (in his year-old capacity of "Principal Surveyor, Entire Pacific Coast") was instrumental in holding both casualties to partial losses, and earned both men Brengle's praise at the 1934 annual meeting.

At the opposite end of this time-span came two strandings which involved the personal attendance of Captain Bull, chief surveyor since 1935. In September, 1940, repeating his *Garfield* exploit of eighteen years before, Bull hurried to St. Croix, Virgin Islands, to represent the Association at the refloating of the cargo liner *Robin Adair*. Four months later he was back in what would shortly become "U-boat Alley," to oversee the refloating of the 705-foot United States Lines passenger ship *Manhattan,* which had suffered the indignity of taking the ground on a moonlit January evening, just off Palm Beach. With the aid of Merritt-Chapman & Scott equipment, she ultimately became one of the largest vessels ever to be pried off a shoal, but her refloating and repair bill was also one of the largest partial losses ever paid by underwriters to that date.

Overshadowing it, however, were two intervening total losses which still rank among the greatest disasters in American maritime history: the *Morro Castle* in 1934, and the *President Hoover* in 1937. Both were new luxury liners, the former one of a 508-foot pair built in 1930 for the Ward Line's New York-Havana service, the latter one of two 654-foot Dollar Line sisters which were the largest passenger ships ever to show the Stars and Stripes on the Pacific. Both required strenuous involvement of Association representatives.

The early morning of September 9, 1934, found Bull speeding by car from New York to Asbury Park, New Jersey, where the charred and smoking ruin of what had been the finest ship in the coastwise and West Indies fleet had just drifted ashore in front of Convention Hall. At three the morning before, shortly after the death of her master, the New York-bound *Morro Castle* had mysteriously burst into flame. In the demoralization and panic that ensued, 134 people died, the vessel was gutted, and heavy weather parted the towline which the Coast Guard Cutter *Tampa* had finally managed to connect.

Fires still blazed throughout the beached hulk when Bull reached it, and days passed before all spaces could be inspected; but the totality of the loss was apparent almost from the first. Sides were bulged and buckled, stanchions twisted, precision machinery wrecked, and all accommodation spaces (in which wood had been extensively used) obliterated. By September 22, Bull gave it as his opinion not only that the ship was a constructive total loss but that refloating, let alone rebuilding, would be so enormously costly that Syndicate "C" would be well advised to disclaim any interest in the tragic shell. This it did, though paying $2,100,000, its largest settlement up to that time. Since the owners had already abandoned the wreck, its removal devolved on the authorities.

The tragedy of the *Morro Castle* was human, the death of the ship herself being comparatively swift. By contrast, the *President Hoover's* tragedy, virtually unmarred by loss of life, was that of a great liner being slowly tortured to death by nature in the aftermath of a probably needless man-made catastrophe. But man also emerges as the hero of the generally dismal piece, in the person of a United States Salvage Association representative who stayed on the scene for two months, struggling at first to save the ship herself, then to preserve what he could of her cargo.

The setting was Hoishoto, a small rocky island to the east of what was then called Formosa, under the already truculent colors of Japan. The first human error was navigational, as the big Manila-bound *Hoover,* feeling her way in thick weather near midnight on December 11, 1937 (December 10, east longitude time), suddenly found herself in the breakers and slid onto the coral with her electric propulsion motors spinning full astern. Her distress calls set in motion a chain of delegation: the Syndicate calling on the Association, which in turn called on the Everett Steamship Company of Shanghai, then its sole agent throughout East Asia, which called on Captain George Anderson, a private surveyor in Hong Kong.

Anderson knew that, in the monsoon season, every hour sharply reduced chances of refloating the liner. Valuable time

Dollar liner *President Hoover* stranded off Hoishoto Island, Formosa, in January, 1938. Seas have already smashed great gaps in the shell at the waterline.

had already been lost. With emergency gear and a hastily assembled crew of Hong Kong coolies, he put to sea on the Dollar Liner *President McKinley,* which anchored off Hoishoto the morning of the thirteenth. There the final blow awaited him—official refusal to admit the coolies and their foremen. Japan would allow none but Japanese salvors to work in her waters. After two more days the salvage tug *Ushu Maru* arrived from Hong Kong; but it was already too late. The weather closed down again, and the ship's fate was sealed.

Anderson's diary of his two months' labor, though technical and matter-of-fact, has a dramatic force which makes it hard to put aside. By December 22 he grimly admitted the ship a constructive total loss, and the Syndicate paid a top-capacity claim of $2,500,000. But at cargo underwriters' request he stayed on, racing the elements to get as much as possible

Two bow-on snapshots, taken by the U. S. Salvage Association representative at the height of a monsoon storm when it was impossible to hold the camera steady, show how they did it.

Salvage ship *Miho Maru* seen from inside the liner's torn hull.

ashore by aerial cables. It became a nightmare, with sights, sounds, and smells all on a heroic scale. Spoiled food in the powerless reefer compartments wrapped everyone in a stench that could almost be seen. Storm after storm rocked the huge hulk in its coral cradle, threatening to break it in two and wrenching off side-plates one by one. Weirdest of all were the huge seas smashing into these holes like giant air-compressors, setting up internal blast effects of dynamite force which tossed steel hatch covers high in the air and catapulted unwary salvors from sideports as if from the pressurized cabin of an aircraft. At least one man drowned.

With the end of the agony approaching and virtually all salvable goods removed, Anderson was released to make his laborious way home, by cart track across the island, the coaster *Menado Maru* to Keelung, and the oceangoing *Hong Kong Maru* to Hong Kong. During his long sojourn at the wreck he had broken out a succession of ensigns from the flag locker, bending on a new one each time its predecessor was whipped to ribbons. The *President Hoover* was still American, having not yet passed to her ultimate owner, the Asiatic Scrap Metal Corporation. Hence, before leaving, February 11, he selected the strongest remaining flag, made it as secure as he could, then paused at the island crest and, with a melodrama certainly foreign to his normal seaman's ways, saluted a dying friend who, four years before Pearl Harbor, had found this a hostile coast.

⚓   ⚓   ⚓

Not all the big ships which claimed Association attention were in trouble. In February, 1935, four months before the French Line's *Normandie* made her New York debut as new queen of the world's oceans, she was the subject of a report by Bull, distributed to underwriters and Association directors, who could not then foresee that within eight years she would become the queen of giant salvage problems. In 1934 a little ship, the "power houseboat *Ava*," had precipitated a different kind of problem when a surveyor apparently more used to

74

steel than wood construction wrote a report in alleged reliance on which she was purchased by the then-flourishing *Pictorial Review*. Subsequent discovery that her hull timbers were seriously decayed resulted in a liability suit by the magazine and an out-of-court settlement of $3,500. This and other uncomfortable experiences of the time helped crystallize the Association's present-day policy against use of its survey reports as warranties of sale.

Casualty attendance apart, the Association's primary preoccupations in the latter thirties arose from revived ship-construction programs, naval and merchant. The attendant resurgence of builder's risk insurance coverage, both by Syndicate "C" and by the newborn Builder's Risk Syndicate, led to a five-year program of shipyard fire-hazard inspections in which the Association collaborated with the Navy, the inspection bureaus of the fire insurance companies, and later the fire-engineering firm of Vlachos & Company, under Bull's coordination. Specifications of yard safety requirements for all naval vessel types were prepared and circulated by him in 1935.

For American shipping and marine underwriting, the outstanding development of the prewar years was passage of the Merchant Marine Act of 1936. The large-scale fleet-replacement program mandated by this legislation should have entailed expanded business for the Syndicate and Association—and ultimately did. But for several years after 1936, Bull made increasingly pessimistic annual reports on the "block obsolescence" of the fleet built under the emergency construction program of 1916-1919 and the absence of replacement construction other than a few tankers. Not until the 1939 meeting did he prophesy that "the coming year, we believe, will begin to see the retirement of the currently operated twenty-year-old war-built tonnage . . . and new ships, better built of better materials, take their place."

His prediction was accurate, so far as it went. One thing he could not foresee was that, before the next meeting, world events would have made the scale of ship production set by the new Maritime Commission glaringly inadequate. Another was that passage of the Neutrality Act would drastically curtail

Two Merritt-Chapman & Scott salvage tugs strain to refloat the *Manhattan,* off Palm Beach in January, 1941 (see p. 70).

American shipping activity on several major trade routes, but stimulate it on others. For the Association, the effect on survey volume would be varied and gradual. While its North European business would suffer disastrously, its overall income in the three years remaining before Pearl Harbor would show increases of 3.8%, 1.6%, and 17.8%, as the nation and its shipping moved toward war.

XI

THE ASSOCIATION AT WAR

By the close of 1940, preparedness for a war which now seemed certain to engulf them had become a general, if reluctant, preoccupation of the American people and Government. The urgency of the times affected all segments of the economy, but none more heavily than the maritime industries. How well prepared was the United States Salvage Association?

Well enough, we can say in retrospect; but not much more than that. It had able men, notably Captain Bull, but was still understaffed and organizationally hampered by the cutbacks of recent years. On balance, its strongest single qualification was that it was still in existence, and therefore available to meet national needs, after surviving its multiple tribulations of the thirties. Except perhaps on the Great Lakes, it was not prospering in 1940. On the west coast it was still essentially a junior partner. Overseas, its promising reorganization of 1936 had virtually collapsed as a result of the Neutrality Act's exclusion of American-flag shipping from most European ports. Its consolidated worldwide results for 1940 were significantly below those for 1936, the year of Brengle's death.

Its expansion having been frustrated by the Depression, the Association was now more definitely than ever a subdepartment of the American Marine Insurance Syndicates. With one exception, its administration rested throughout the war upon men who were primarily Syndicate officers. Harwood was president, under his broad contract to manage all Syndicate activities. Two of the "founding fathers," Hedge and McComb, served as his vice presidents during the early months, but each died shortly after completing his term. Vice president at the war's end was Donald C. Bowersock of the Providence Washington Insurance Company. The Syndicates' treasurer and

Captain George S. Bull, who joined Syndicate "A" in 1920, became Deputy Chief Surveyor in 1930, and served as Chief Surveyor, 1935-1950.

Courtesy Mr. John S. Bull

secretary, Schuler and Adams, held the same titles in the Association, the latter being succeeded on his death in 1944 by S. Donald Livingston. Oliver J. DuFour, manager of the Syndicate's Loss Department, was by the very nature of his duties closely involved in Association matters.

This left McAlinden the only Association officer *per se,* outside the Surveying Department. Eight months before Pearl Harbor, he became executive secretary, his former post of manager being abolished as Harwood assumed most managerial functions himself.

The technical staff, under Bull as chief surveyor, included such men of long experience and recognized ability as P. S. Jolly, Andrew S. Varni, and John Rohde in New York, and, in the three surviving exclusive offices, John E. Tull at Boston, James T. Christie at Norfolk, and Guy A. Myers at Cleveland. Also enhancing Association prestige, though currently serving as agents only, were John Mitchell at Baltimore, William Freeman at New Orleans, and George Alden in London.

The retrenchments of the thirties had, however, left the organization undermanned in this vital area. Recognizing this, as early as the fall of 1939, Harwood cited a need for younger men—all but two of the surveyors just listed having joined the Association between 1920 and 1927. Efforts in this direction soon collided head-on with mounting Selective Service demands, and for the duration it became less a matter of finding new apprentice manpower than of holding on to young talent already on the payroll. Fortunately, the Association's specialized capability was in short enough supply and long enough demand by both naval and shipping agencies to permit generally successful if hard bargaining for draft deferment of essential staff.

Association financing in 1940, and indeed throughout the war, also suggested complete subordination and a more restricted scope of operation than the national emergency would ultimately require. Since the termination of the Shipping Board agreement in 1931, Syndicate "A"—or more specifically its subscribing companies—had been the sole source of any funds needed to balance fee income and operating cost. These syndicate subscribers still owned the Association through the medium of 2,000 shares carried on the books at five dollars each. In addition, they had provided, in proportion to their shareholding, a revolving fund of $125,000 to underwrite Association needs. From this and other assets, Syndicate "A" made advances in the form of loans to the operating organization. It maintained bank accounts and safe deposit boxes in its own name, and invested monies not currently needed in government securities.

By mid-October, 1942, when a sweeping reorganization of the Syndicate-Association structure was in the planning stages, this investment stood at $50,000; the Association's indebtedness, at $70,000. But abnormal wartime conditions were already putting former methods of financing under severe stress. A number of companies had withdrawn from the Syndicates as a result of disastrous submarine losses that spring, leading the Finance Committee to complain that "no satisfactory mechanics exist.

for replacing" their share of the revolving fund. In addition, the Maritime Commission and its War Shipping Administration, now about to become the Association's largest clients, were falling into a chronic state of delinquency in remitting for services rendered.

Syndicate "A" dealt with the immediate situation by a sale of securities and an emergency advance of $5,000 to the Association. However, succeeding months made it increasingly clear that entirely new funding would be called for, both by the conditions of the time and by the reorganization plan, under which Syndicates "A," "B," and "C" were to be liquidated and the United States Salvage Association left for the first time—on paper, at least—without a parent organization.

The reorganization became effective December 1, 1943. Its most conspicuous effect was to create one surviving underwriting group, the American Marine Hull Insurance Syndicate (the "Marine" was dropped thirteen years later). The subscribers to former Syndicate "C" became the subscribers to the new Syndicate. Also preserved was the United States Salvage Association, whose indebtedness to expiring Syndicate "A" was resolved by a superficially complicated plan which, reduced to its essentials, consisted of the Association's underwriter owners buying themselves out. The subscribers to the new Syndicate readjusted the ownership basis "through the sale and purchase of stock among themselves" and subscribed proportionately to an issue of 2½% Association debentures the proceeds of which, less those from the sale of Syndicate "A" securities, satisfied all book obligations and gave the Association an operating base for the future. Syndicate "A" was pronounced liquidated June 15, 1944.

Though nominally independent, however, the Association was still a *de facto* instrumentality of the underwriting syndicate, exclusively owned by Syndicate subscribers and administered (McAlinden excepted) by Syndicate officers. Sporadic consideration was given throughout the war to broadening the Association's scope and effectiveness by modifying its traditional and deliberate non-profit status to "enable the building up of surplus reserves." This was rejected, on advice of counsel, in

Freighter *Delisle*   Liberty ship *George S. Wasson*

Torpedo and mine damage to four ships attended by Association surveyors.

Tanker *Oklahoma*   Tanker *Malay*

October, 1942, March, 1944, and October, 1944, as against "the Association's best interests," even where the object was to build up "a postwar development fund." The organization's success in meeting the heavy wartime demands of the national and allied cause is truly surprising in view of the organizational and financial guidelines under which it had to operate.

Ready or not, it was plain by the fall of 1941 that the United States Salvage Association had a landslide of business on its hands. Surveys, which in 1940 had shown a modest increase of 88 over 1939, with only $3,000 added income, now took a jump of 556, to 4,011. Income for the year was up $33,000, to $218,000. This growth rate was more than doubled in 1942, the year which saw the steepest percentage increases of the war, (29.9% in number of surveys, 35.3% in income). Shouldering this workload, much of it of an emergency nature, probably made this the most hectic of the war years for the Association.

There was to be no let-up. It became almost ritual for McAlinden to report at each annual meeting that the year just past had been the largest in the organization's history. From 5,209 surveys in 1942, the score rose to 6,373 in 1943, 7,360 in 1944, and 7,667 in 1945. Annual income climbed from $295,000 to $426,000. Overall expansion from the 1939 base was 128% in surveys held, 134% in income. The effectiveness of wartime anti-inflation controls, by the way, is strikingly shown by contrasting these nearly equivalent percentages with those for the five postwar years, in which surveys decreased over 21% while dollar income rose almost 9%.

The main factor in the wartime increase was of course work performed for the Government, especially the War Shipping Administration; though this was not at once apparent. For the month of September, 1942, McAlinden's clientele breakdown was: underwriting syndicates, 40%; WSA, 20%; "other interests," 40%. In presenting the 1943 results, however, he said, "The increase is all survey work which came to the Association for the War Shipping Administration's account." With that agency in full control of ocean shipping, and with many harbor and inland movements under other governmental auspices, it is remarkable that private employment held as nearly level as it did.

A large early block of war work was performance of condition surveys on ships being requisitioned by the Government, a fleet which grew rapidly after June, 1941. It was still being added to when German torpedoes and mines began making large-scale subtractions in early 1942. The nature of the U-boats' tactics, and the slimness of naval protection, meant that too often the victims did not survive to reach surveyors' hands; but, as a growing number of cripples made port, a new class of damage survey work developed.

It was strenuous work, and hazardous. The surveyor boarding a casualty might be in as great danger as the men who had sailed her. Three tankers attended in middle Atlantic ports offered the Association's men something less than cruise ship amenities. One, an Atlantic Refining Company vessel which made Chesapeake Bay with nothing apparently holding her together except her bottom plating, had to be lightered of her full lading of "casinghead gas" in a hair-raising anchorage operation whereby salt water was pumped into the bottom of her tanks to force cargo out of the top, while the monstrous risk of sparks from her grinding plates was prayerfully met by dumping drums of foam extinguisher into the five-foot gap in her deck. A Sinclair Oil carrier beached in flames at Morehead City, North Carolina, finally burned herself out about two weeks later and was boarded by an Association surveyor, who made the chilling discovery that beneath her buckled decks, which had evidently been red hot from bow to stern, were four tanks still full of usable gasoline. A Gulf Oil ship made Wilmington, North Carolina, with a large hole blown out of the bottom of two forward tanks and, for lack of even temporary repair capacity at that port, had to be dispatched under her own power on a frightening voyage to Baltimore yards. Yet all these mutilated craft were duly surveyed, repaired to specifications, and returned to service.

Risky as it was, this was vitally important work, not only because of the values involved but because of the critical need to preserve and utilize every possible ton of shipping capacity.

The *E. H. Blum,* then one of the world's largest tankers, and soon to be the Hull Syndicate's heaviest war loss, upon her delivery in 1941.

Courtesy Mariners Museum

What remained of the *Blum* on February 26, 1942, after mining and stranding.

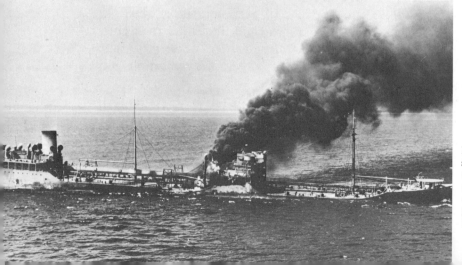

In sight of the southern beach a torpedoed tanker, not yet supplied with guns for her tub burns and settle

Author's collect

It was not always successful, as, for example, in the case of the vessel which became the Hull Syndicate's costliest war loss, the tanker *E. H. Blum*. This brand-new 19,405-deadweight-ton ship, mined in February, 1942, off the Virginia Capes, came heartbreakingly close to reaching safety, Charles Auld recalls, only to strand and break in two near Cape Henry. With Association attendance, her bow was ultimately towed in, but she was ruled a total loss—a heavier one for the Syndicate than the *President Hoover*.

While this U-Boat blitz raged, and until WSA assumed full responsibility for war risk insurance, Syndicate service remained paramount. Harwood reflected this when he said of the Association early in 1942, "We rely more than ever on this organization to give us technical services and advice." From midyear on, however, negotiations were underway between underwriters and Washington that would eventuate in the Wartimehull Agreement, under which, in 1944-1945, WSA became directly or indirectly the Association's principal customer for the duration. Both condition and damage surveys on the government-controlled fleet were required, and the build-up involved was forecast by McAlinden September 16, 1943, when he said, "We will soon be called upon to begin inspection of 600 or more oceangoing vessels." Such inspection continued "a substantial part of the increase in surveys" during 1944.

A significant shift was taking place meanwhile in the subject matter of damage surveys. With the tightening of convoy protection, Bull could report early in 1944 that "major damages due to enemy action . . . have all but disappeared." However, collision, stranding, and other injury resulting from the black-out conditions of wartime navigation was increasingly frequent.

Long before WSA business reached its peak, the Association was strenuously engaged in work for other Government agencies, notably damage survey contracts with the Navy and Coast Guard. Much of this work (a byproduct of which was to aid retention of skilled personnel otherwise vulnerable to the draft) continued throughout hostilities, and even into the postwar years under a late-1945 contract with the Navy's Judge Advo-

85

cate General's Office ("JAG") "to act for them worldwide if necessary on damage to privately-owned vessels."

War pressures were such by 1943 as to put an end to the Association's only official involvement in cargo surveying outside the Great Lakes district. This was an arrangement dating from the early twenties whereby surveyor Christie at Norfolk acted for The Board of Underwriters of New York in the loading inspection of coal, that port's chief prewar commodity, and one whose inspection could be readily combined with survey of the carrying vessel. The huge wartime importance of Hampton Roads as a naval and shipping center so multiplied Christie's hull responsibilities that the New York Board was asked to install its own loading inspector, "making our office his headquarters."

The Association's wartime vicissitudes in North America were as nothing compared to the radical fluctuations of fortune experienced by its "advance post" in London. Alden and his understudy, Ganly, were just managing to extricate the General European Agency from the loss column when, as previously recorded, the outbreak of war and the clamp-down of the Neutrality Act on American ship movements all but destroyed their operation. Before the conflict in Europe was a month old, prospective financial losses loomed so large as to dictate a 37½% cut in the guarantee under which Alden had worked since 1936, Ganly's transfer to New York, and stringent office economies. But the situation worsened steadily, with British costs and taxes rising as Alden's business fell. To his plea for relief at the end of 1940, the directors replied suggesting he return home to take a job they had tentatively arranged with the American Bureau of Shipping.

It would have proved a disaster for the Association had he done so. Within weeks he and his office were to be of pivotal importance in the organization's impending war effort. Surveys for Association account, of which he had been able to report only 22 in 1940 and 7 in 1941, soared in the next four years to 137, 537, 1,010, and finally 1,317. By March, 1943, Harwood said, "Mr. Alden's work in the past two years has been carried out under extreme difficulties and his services throughout the

British Isles have been not only of great value in connection with survey matters but of inestimable help to the United States Maritime Commission and War Shipping Administration."

As the Normandy invasion approached, Association expertise was drawn upon, in both London and New York, for technical service and advice in connection with the vast quantity and variety of shipping involved, and especially the elaborate cross-channel and transatlantic towing operations required. These came to be a specialty of Bull, who had supervised the towing of base equipment to Greenland in 1940 and is credited with devising procedures and overseeing preparation of more than 100 wartime tows, among them the delivery of floating drydocks from the Gulf Coast to the South Pacific and of dredges to restore the harbor at Guam while American seizure of the Marianas was still being consolidated.

His prime contribution, however, was to the towage logistics of the Atlantic war, and particularly to meeting the exactions of "Operation Overlord." These were matters for which Rear Admiral Edmond J. Moran then bore the responsibility on General Eisenhower's staff. One of Moran's hardest planning problems was how to meet General Bradley's heavy tonnage requirement of beach-landed supplies for the opening phase of this unprecedented amphibious assault. No suitable self-propelled vessels were available, and virtually all towable equipment in the United Kingdom was already fully committed.

Moran suggested to Bull that the only suitable vessel available in sufficient numbers was the standard New York harbor carfloat, an overlength decked barge designed to transport three strings of freight cars. Unfortunately, these craft were all on the wrong side of the ocean, and their design seemed to preclude successful delivery overseas. But the Association's chief surveyor soon worked out a solution to this problem. Single carfloats might be ruled out, but *two* carfloats, one on top of the other, would constitute a vessel of sufficient depth and seaworthiness to face the Atlantic crossing.

Moran approved the program in England and, under Bull's supervision in New York, a procession of requisitioned

Grimly testifying to the hazards of blackout operation, the *North King* rests in drydock June 6, 1943, after colliding with the *Empire Pibroch*.

The Normandy beachhead in June, 1944, with a Seabee repair shop in the foreground, blockships and "Mulberry" caissons in the background, and in the right middle distance what appears to be one of Capt. Bull's New York harbor carfloats.

Courtesy Rear Adm. Edmond J. Moran

carfloats were hustled into drydocks and sunk, so that their mates could be floated in and welded on top to form solid "doubledeckers." Within weeks the first group tow, comprising fifty tug and barge units, was dispatched on its successful crossing. Separated in England, these and their successors became carfloats again and were ready by D-Day to make the Normandy beaches the remotest railhead ever reached by the Lackawanna, the Lehigh Valley, and the Jersey Central.

The close working relationship thus cemented continued throughout the war, with Bull masterminding (Admiral Moran's word) all technical projects on the New York end. Twenty-six years after VE-Day, the Admiral summed up the Association's contribution to hastening that triumphant occasion: "If we hadn't had the United States Salvage Association, my end would have been a disaster. With Bull here, there was no trouble."

Meanwhile in London, Alden, though heavily occupied late in 1944 with assisting WSA, the Army Transport Service, and American ships' agents in the reopened continental ports, also devoted much attention to planning the postwar rehabilitation of Association agency facilities throughout Europe. He visited New York in January, 1945, to discuss prospects, and was authorized, "as these ports are liberated," to "select the best surveying talent . . . on a temporary basis, leaving the general set-up of agencies to be discussed at a later time."

Having entered the war period as a subordinate and understrength organization, it is not surprising that the Association's role throughout was less that of a single, sharply-defined working entity than that of an indispensable technological resource in short supply, to be drawn upon, as the national interest might dictate, by a wide range of employers. That these were mainly governmental was inevitable, and is attested by the fact that, in the first postwar year, survey volume decreased 18% overall, and 82% in the London office. Yet by extraordinary and dedicated effort the huge wartime volume was dealt with. How it was done is best described in Harwood's tribute at the 1945 annual meeting: "The volume of work done by the Association during the past year has been accomplished only because of the fact that the surveyors have worked practically every night and quite often Saturdays and Sundays. Being out on surveys so much of the time during the day, they have had to write up their reports outside of office hours." He concluded "that the Association was most fortunate in the personnel of the staff."

WILLIAM BRADFORD HARWOOD
President of the Association, 1938-1950

XII

POSTWAR REGROUPMENT

I T might be supposed that the experience of having to meet war's demands with an undermanned organization which had been running in second gear for a decade would have led to immediate postwar enlargement of size and scope. Speculation as to why it did not is probably fruitless, but it is likely that the Association's very success in coping with crisis, under the strong leadership of such men as Harwood and Bull, tended to obscure for the stockholders the fact that success had been achieved in spite of inadequate facilities, not because of them. Certain it is that another five years were to pass before the inevitable, long-overdue expansion began.

There were straws in the wind, however. Despite the sharp falling-off of survey volume and income in 1946, neither fell anywhere near prewar levels, even in the London office. On the contrary, income climbed irregularly but steadily from 1947 on, while the Association's average survey total was double that of the pre-Pearl Harbor years.

The Navy "JAG" agreement, already referred to, was another foretaste of developments to come: first in a series of contracts with public, military and civilian agencies which would build both income and prestige for the organization in the fifties and sixties.

But the routine fare of the times was still condition and damage surveying of Syndicate-insured vessels, the first category swelled initially by merchant tonnage returning from war service to "civilian life"; the second, by the structural defects and weaknesses which standard ships of war construction were displaying in, at times, epidemic volume. As to the former, the Association late in 1945 replied to a WSA query that it would survey vessels redelivered by that agency to their owners at "usual commercial rates and not subject to renegotiation." A very sizable body of private tonnage was involved in this project, with tankers already being released from requisition, and dry-cargo vessels due to follow in the early months of 1946.

A conspicuous source of damage work, even during the war, was structural failure of welded hulls. The Maritime Commission, the American Bureau of Shipping, and the Association all devoted intense study to the problem, and reinforcement by "strapping" was successively prescribed for the various standard types. In March, 1946, Bull expressed premature gratification that such failures were apparently decreasing. He was then "inclined to think that this may be due to less all around abuse of the kind ships were subjected to during the war years," but in 1948 he reported the fractures continuing, even to some ships already strapped. The trouble persisted into the fifties, with Association surveyors never getting to inspect some of the gravest cases, such as the *Southern Districts, Pennsylvania,* and *Washington Mail,* which broke up and sank in stormy seas.

Other recurrent weaknesses which taxed Association talent to devise not merely remedial but preventive measures through the forties included tailshaft and rudder assembly failures, especially on Liberty Ships, and main motor generator breakdowns on T2 tankers. An abnormal incidence of heavy weather damage, strandings, collisions and fires in 1946-1947 also worried (and provided work for) the Association. Conceding by implication that war conditions were not the only ones conducive to ship abuse, Bull thought this outbreak might "have its cause in the handling of the ships by immature, inexperienced personnel."

As a primary obligation to its underwriter owners, the Association still kept a close check on repair cost trends, an essential factor in loss prediction and rate-making. Bull reported regularly on existing cost levels and his estimate of their movement in the year ahead, and he was rarely far out. It has today been axiomatic for almost a generation that repair costs *never* go down, only up; but these closing years of the forties gave him one last chance to prophesy in terms sweet to underwriters'

Stern section of the *Fort Mercer* wallows off Cape Cod in the seas that killed her.
Courtesy Moran Towing & Transportation Co.

The stern of the *Bridgewater* shelters at Fremantle, Western Australia, after being finally towed in from the Indian Ocean (see p. 156).

ears. Of course, the dip came in the wake of enormous increases: he estimated that at the end of 1945 repairs cost 100% more than in 1939, and accurately forecast that in each of the two ensuing years they would rise 20% more. But by the 1949 annual meeting, with shipyard activity down and competition up, he foresaw "no further increase in ship repair costs," and the next year he could confirm that they had actually dropped 10%. His retirement before the 1951 meeting spared him from having to report that they had started up again.

⚓ ⚓ ⚓

The field organization at this period, while generally workable and active, already displayed certain weaknesses and illogicalities inherited from the economy drive of the thirties. The breakdown into only three "exclusive" branch offices and a number of agencies, supposedly on the basis of business regionally available, no longer made sense in light of the average volume reported for these assorted operating units during the five postwar years. The home office in New York and the Great Lakes office headed the list, but next in order were two agencies, Mitchell's at Baltimore and Freeman's at New Orleans, while one of the regular offices, Boston, ranked next to last, reporting fewer surveys than either London or the other overseas agencies lumped together.

It is said that some of the more experienced and successful surveyors who had previously been converted to agents preferred to stay agents, and had no wish to revert to salaried status, which they were convinced, probably rightly, would be less remunerative than an arrangement where they could skim much of the cream of "outside" work, so long as they did not slight their primary obligation to the Association. But it could no longer be pretended that Baltimore and New Orleans were minor sources of work when the former had built from a 1946 total of 330 surveys to a five-year average of 634; the latter from 343 to 507—superior records to that of the Norfolk exclusive office, which had climbed only from 438 to a 509 average.

The Cleveland office, though it showed a slight net decline in these years, was by all odds the leader in survey volume outside New York. Setting aside government work, in which New York had a heavy edge, average annual output totals were only 127 apart: 1829 surveys for New York to 1702 for Cleveland. Though Great Lakes practices and distances meant that a higher proportion of this freshwater work was actually performed by "outside" fee surveyors than in the coastal ports, it is obvious that after twenty years the Association's inland venture was in thriving condition.

Boston, San Francisco, Galveston, and London all presented special problems in the late forties, most of them not fully resolved until the fifties. At Boston the 25-year regime of John E. Tull as resident surveyor ended with his illness and retirement in 1946. A reserved man with a reputation of going by the book, Tull probably commanded more respect than affection, but he was indispensably valuable to the organization in the Northeast, notably after the New England Hurricane of 1938 and throughout the war. Beatrice Dobbins, who recently retired after 43 years' service at Boston, says he was "of the 'old school,' very strict, but an excellent surveyor."

Upon his incapacitation, Mrs. Dobbins was placed in administrative charge at Boston and retained that position (actual surveys being handled by men detailed from New York) for some months while it was debated whether to reduce or possibly close the office. This was the most responsible position yet assigned a woman in Association history, and was suitably recalled at the time of her retirement ceremonies in 1970.

The difficulties at Boston were a consequence of that port's steady decline in recent decades, which the war and the demise of Atlantic coastwise shipping had accelerated. Competing private surveyors had also claimed an increasing share of the port's decimated international shipping. Two counterbalancing factors were the fishing boat work which Boston had handled in increasing volume ever since 1921 and a rising quantity of yacht surveys since the immediate prewar years. In the end, the Association board ruled late in 1946 that the Boston office should be retained and "a suitable man" installed there. Tull was then replaced by John G. Bisset, who was succeeded two years later by William S. Henry. Bisset later served the Asso-

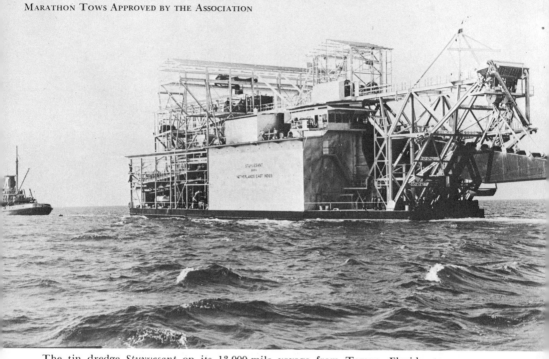

The tin dredge *Stuyvesant* on its 13,000-mile voyage from Tampa, Florida, to Banka in the East Indies, March, 1947, towed by the *Watch Hill.*

Courtesy Moran Towing & Transportation Co.

The floating power plant *Resistance* being maneuvered for the main leg of its 11,000-mile journey from Portsmouth, New Hampshire, to Pusan, Korea, in 1961 (see p. 169) .

Jeff Blinn photo

ciation until his death in 1969 as resident surveyor at Los Angeles.

West coast arrangements, unchanged since before the war and destined to remain so until the early fifties, warrant mention at this point only because the poor record of these years, when practically every other area was expanding its business, exposed the failure of the San Francisco set-up to generate significant survey volume for Association account. Apart from one wartime year, private surveys never surpassed two figures, and for the years 1946-1950 they averaged only 71, barely one-third of Boston's poor showing. Government work formed a higher proportion of the total than elsewhere: of the sparse 1,489 surveys reported in two decades following the Gatewood agreement 660, or 44%, fell in this category.

The Texas coast, described by McAlinden as "always somewhat of a trouble spot for us," was another area in which, for over fifteen years, only agency representation had been maintained. Despite this it was one of only two areas to show steadily improving results from 1946 to 1950. The period's only important change in regional organization took place here at the end of 1949, when agency headquarters were shifted from their historic base at Galveston to the fast-rising sister port of Houston. This change and the retention of Boston were accompanied by the now-familiar plea for greater stockholder utilization of Association capacity.

The problem of London was the thorniest of all. It was purely economic, with postwar conditions mirroring on a magnified scale the squeeze in which Alden had found himself back in Neutrality Act days. After his war performance, no one questioned the Association's need of him; but the imponderables were great and, with British taxes rising, postwar business unquestionably falling, and Sterling devaluation threatened, periodic increases in his guarantee proved only stopgaps. Finally the perplexed directors dispatched Clifford G. Cornwell, Harwood's recently recruited assistant, to explore the problem on the scene.

Cornwell's exhaustive report, in May, 1949, proposed guidelines for future Association operation in Europe. It con-

97

firmed the necessity of retaining the London headquarters (chiefly for its proximity to major insurance markets and despite a significant rise in continental business which might soon require an operating sub-base at Antwerp or Rotterdam) and of retaining Alden as general agent. To extricate him from seeming financial quicksands, it recommended converting his guarantee from pounds to dollars. For various reasons, including his own preference, it advised continuing him as an agent rather than an employee.

However, in mapping future European organization, Cornwell advised immediate appointment of a salaried assistant (who turned out to be Ganly) and conversion of the agency to an exclusive branch office at the termination of Alden's contract. These recommendations were approved and thus, by 1950, the groundwork had at last been laid for the sort of direct overseas operation which had been envisioned, and set aside, by Syndicate "A" thirty years before.

⚓   ⚓   ⚓

In New York, this period of postwar readjustment was marked by an abnormally high rate of executive turnover, amounting virtually to a clean sweep of the Association's wartime direction. Though much of this was coincidental and a natural sequel to an emergency period in which everyone had felt an obligation to stay at his post, it unquestionably facilitated the new departures of the early fifties by allowing them to be guided by individuals relatively unencumbered with prior concepts and routines.

It was unwritten practice to elect a new vice president from insurance company ranks every other year, but in this brief span of time the last wartime vice president, Bowersock, had four successors: Martin W. Morron of the Aetna, John S. Gilbertson of the Hartford Fire, Leslie J. Haefner of the Fireman's Fund, and J. Arthur Bogardus of the Atlantic Mutual. In addition, the three years from the end of 1947 to the end of 1950 brought the retirement of three key officers who held parallel positions in the Syndicate and Association: Ernest W. Schuler, the treasurer, in 1947; Oliver J. DuFour, the Loss

Department manager, in 1949; and, in 1950, W. Bradford Harwood who, as Syndicate chairman and Association president, had held a taut managerial rein on both organizations for a dozen demanding years.

On the surveying side, 1950 was a year of severe loss to the Association, with Captain Bull's retirement, 30 years after joining Syndicate "A," and the sudden death of his deputy and anticipated successor, John Rohde. Whatever changes might be impending, they would not be made by anyone who had been on the "first team" at the time of Pearl Harbor.

Most replacements were already on deck, however, headed by Cornwell, whom Harwood had brought to the Syndicate from the United States Maritime Commission in 1947. Schuler's place was taken by Romer F. Weyant; DuFour's, by Samuel Gore. Andrew S. Varni assumed the senior surveying responsibility.

But the most noteworthy change and, by general acceptance, a major turning point in the Association's history was the creation at Cornwell's instance of a new position of General Manager of the United States Salvage Association, and the appointment to it in January, 1951, of the man who would initiate and guide a new era of expansion, J. Paul Thompson.

XIII

THE SHIFT INTO HIGH GEAR

THE exact halfway point of the twentieth century, midnight December 31, 1950, brought to the United States Salvage Association a change of command which would set in motion a complete new order of organization and operation. For the first time since 1931, a radical alteration of course was about to be made.

At that date and hour Clifford G. Cornwell succeeded to the Association presidency. His succession was not sudden, having been determined far enough in advance to permit deliberate long-term planning.

As we have seen, the Association had been virtually stripped of its wartime leadership in a space of three years. Seizing this opportunity, Cornwell urged upon the board of directors, in the fall of 1950, that the time had again come when administrative direction should be vested in an Association officer appointed exclusively for that purpose. His own primary duties as Harwood's successor would henceforth be Syndicate underwriting and management, and, though he would retain the presidency, he believed that someone else, preferably a nonunderwriter, should be in immediate charge of Association affairs.

His choice, confirmed by the Syndicate and Association boards on December 21, 1950, fell upon J. Paul Thompson, a 52-year-old Californian marine engineer and a former surveyor for the American Bureau of Shipping. Thompson had gone to sea at the age of sixteen as an oiler in Army transports. Gaining his chief engineer's license seven years later, he had subsequently held increasingly responsible positions with some of the major American steamship companies, including a period in the twenties as "resident inspector" aboard the giant *Leviathan.*

CLIFFORD G. CORNWELL
President of the Association, 1951-1957
Chairman, 1958-1970

During the war and until 1948 he had been an executive with the Matson Navigation Company, where his generally technical assignments ranged from port engineer at Honolulu and San Francisco to president of the United Engineering Company, Matson's maintenance subsidiary, and manager of construction and repair for the parent company. His appointment to the newly-created post of general manager marked an explicit return to the concept of technological Association direction for the first time since Gatewood's brief tenure twenty years before.

Thompson's first project upon taking office January 8,

1951, was to survey existing organization and staff, evaluate its adequacy to handle Association responsibilities, current and potential, and evolve what presently came to be known as the "Organization Program." He had the backing of a special committee of directors comprising J. Arthur Bogardus, Percy Chubb, II, and Robert R. Dwelly. To this committee on March 2 he submitted an ambitious plan of functional and staff expansion, accompanied by proposed organization charts and an admittedly steep price tag (over twelve percent of the Association's entire 1950 income). The board adopted this plan in its entirety the same month.

The reasons given for this unqualified support were significant and refreshing. The committee found it "in the interest of the Salvage Association, of the Syndicate, and of the American hull market in general that the operating effectiveness of the Salvage Association be stepped up." Besides recognizing the new pressures created by the Korean War and the strong competing "demands for technical personnel arising out of the reactivated defense program," it observed that, quite apart from special jobs required by that program, the Association's regular workload had attained "overwhelming" proportions. It concurred in Thompson's view "that a proper staffing . . . can save the American market the additional cost many times over through savings in damage repair costs"—always a telling argument with the stockholders. But perhaps its cleanest break with the perfunctory attitudes of the past was its assertion that it was "firmly of the belief that it is the duty of the Salvage Association not only to the American insurance market but also to American shipowners and to the Maritime Administration to put itself in first-class working condition to meet the demands which may be anticipated in the predictable future."

Two things were now amply clear: that the Association's underwriter owners recognized that their own interests dictated a much broader technical mission for the organization in the fifties than in any earlier period, and that they discerned in the new general manager the vision and the drive which could bring this mission to pass.

Like most organization charts, those proposed by Thompson were never completely fleshed out, but they are worth scanning as indications of his main developmental ideas. There were two charts: one for immediate adoption, the second depicting a later stage of expansion not explicitly scheduled. The most novel feature of both was a separate technical office under a qualified specialist, to review and analyze survey reports from the field, make systematic studies of accident causation, and handle special projects. On the first chart its director was shown as a "technical assistant" to the general manager.

The lower half of the chart showed four operating departments, two existing and two new. "Office Administration" remained the province of the executive secretary, McAlinden, and "Outside" offices embraced the three exclusive branches and the agencies, domestic and foreign. The other two boxes covered a newly-created office of "Principal Surveyor, New York Area," and a proposed office of "Salvage Operations and Towing." The latter, which seems to have contemplated an active entry of the Association into the "salvage business" *per se*, was never implemented; the former was a geographical scaling-down of the previous office of chief surveyor, other functions of which were now assigned to the technical assistant or reserved for the general manager. It was planned "at a later date" to expand the New York area job to a principal surveyorship for an Atlantic district, on a par with Gulf, Pacific, and Great Lakes districts. Except on the Lakes, however, this plan was not put into effect for some years.

The remainder of 1951 was marked by staff enlargement and upgrading unprecedented in the history of the Association. Under newly approved manning and salary scales, six junior surveyors were employed, and older employees appropriately adjusted and advanced. The most significant new appointment was that of E. P. Pulliam, a 1918 Naval Academy graduate and former marine engineering executive, as technical assistant. Varni, since Rohde's death the ranking New York Office surveyor, was named principal surveyor for the area.

To deal systematically with the enlarged repair cost control problems arising from enlarged operations, Thompson set up in the New York office in 1952 an Estimating Department under Thomas F. Walsh, an experienced shipyard estimator, who continues in charge of this phase of the Association's work today. Believed unique among surveying organizations, this department, through examination and analysis of thousands of surveyors' reports from every part of the globe, can furnish underwriters reliable cost advice, free of the guesswork often found in this field. It compiles for Association stockholders a valuable annual "Recapitulation of Negotiated Cases," showing cost levels on a regional basis, and has been notably helpful to shipowners and the Maritime Administration in collecting world repair cost figures, a program more fully treated in Chapter XV. It has also become a sort of "estimating school" for junior surveyors, of whom perhaps a hundred have been assigned to it for temporary training duty over the years.

In all, between January 1, 1951, and September 30, 1954, employment in the home office exactly doubled—from 19 to 38 —while payroll increased in a somewhat greater ratio: from $96,850 to $209,900. During the same period, however, annual survey income increased from $466,281 to $883,399. Moreover, a committee appointed to examine the entire program, when slack results for 1954 raised misgivings that the Association might have to pass the dividend on its preferred stock, found the augmented scale of operation fully justified in terms of long-range return to the ownership.

It cited, among positive gains to underwriters, improved control over repair costs, facilitation of claims settlements as a result of standardized survey and report procedures, and more effective measures for enforcing adherence to ship repair specifications. Much of this had been made possible by the establishment, under Pulliam, of the Technical Section to perform detailed review of surveys, costs, and research, as well as to develop a coding system for machine analysis, storage, and retrieval of data from a multitude of reports. The Section's existence had also made it possible to undertake a wide range of special studies for underwriters, shipowners, and the Government.

The committee concluded that "results attained under the

J. PAUL THOMPSON
General Manager of the Association, 1951-1957
President, 1958-1963

expanded program appeared to justify the increase in operating cost involved, and that, on the basis of such conclusion, the scope and objectives of the Association, as now constituted, should be reaffirmed." The directors ratified this vote of confidence in Thompson's program on the next-to-last day of 1954.

The very financial worries which had prompted this investigation were themselves occasioned by another forward step taken by the Association early in the Thompson regime. This was the much-discussed, much-postponed departure from the strictly nonprofit, "break-even" basis on which it had operated since 1921.

The recurrent agitation during the forties for a change in this practice was finally brought to a head by the approaching maturity, on January 1, 1954, of the 2½% debentures issued in the process of liquidating Syndicate "A" a decade before. Having in view this $100,000 obligation, a like indebtedness incurred over the years by continued borrowing from the Hull Syndicate, and the expanding Association's crying need for working capital, the stockholders voted in December, 1953, to abandon the old basis with its unrealistic bookkeeping acrobatics and to substitute whatever system was needed "to produce a moderate profit and allow some accumulation of surplus to provide for normal growth." Their new philosophy was "that efficiency and economy of operation will be promoted if management is required to test its expenditures on the basis of the profits which such expenditures will produce."

The means adopted were threefold: (1) exchanging for the maturing debentures a new issue of 5% callable preferred stock, par for par; (2) assessing the holders of the 2,000 outstanding common shares $70 per share, over and above their nominal initial investment of $5 per share; (3) revising the schedule of fees for damage surveys as necessary to counter the existing operating deficit. The capitalization thus attained would permit accounts to be squared with both debenture-holders and Syndicate, and still leave a working fund of about $50,000, believed adequate to current needs and hopefully, with the increase in fee income, to the expense of enlarging West Coast operations, which was already under negotiation.

Three months later, the United States Salvage Association adopted its first budget and became, in greatly increased measure, master of its own economic fate. So well did the new financing work out, despite the misgivings of mid-1954, that the Association was able to call for redemption on May 1, 1957, the entire issue of preferred stock.

⚓ ⚓ ⚓

Between 1951 and 1957 the vice presidents elected to serve with Cornwell were John T. Byrne, Frank B. Zeller, Percy Chubb, II, and Miles F. York. Senior staff losses by retirement during the same period included Charles A. Auld, resident surveyor of the Norfolk office, on August 1, 1952, after 25 years' employment and a previous year as agent at Miami; Andrew S. Varni, principal surveyor of the New York area, on July 1, 1953, after 26 years in the home office; and Michael F. McAlinden, executive secretary, on December 31, 1954, after over a quarter-century of service. At the subsequent annual meeting McAlinden was thanked by Thompson for "assistance and guidance during my short period in the Association."

Several younger staff members already on deck at the time of these departures must be mentioned here because of the active roles they would play in the impending build-up. Senior in point of employment was William S. Henry, a 1938 Webb Institute graduate who joined the Association at the start of 1949 and, as we have seen, was almost immediately placed in charge of the Boston office. He was to return in 1954 to New York, where he would serve as area principal surveyor from 1956 until he resigned in 1958 to enter private practice.

Employed as "surveyor (in training)" the same year as Henry was William F. Watkins, a 1942 graduate of the Massachusetts Institute of Technology, who would serve the organization almost 14 years, all of them in the New York office. Though he never held the title of Principal Surveyor for the New York area, he exercised the responsibilities of that position in 1953-1956. His title at the end of the decade was chief engineer.

Harry S. Townsend, trained at the University of Michigan in naval architecture and marine engineering, joined the Association a year after Watkins. He returned to the Midwest early in 1951, but rejoined the organization late in 1952 and will be heard of at every later stage of its history.

XIV

FROM SEA TO SEA—AT LAST

A MAIN objective of the Organization Program was to broaden and strengthen the Association's field organization. After two decades with nothing but agency representation anywhere in the world outside a triangle bounded by Norfolk, Boston, and Cleveland (or at Baltimore within that triangle), Cornwell and Thompson strongly believed that no expansion program could succeed without a direct Association presence in every major port area frequented by American, and American-insured, ships. It would take a dozen years to accomplish this, but they started at once.

Cornwell, indeed, addressed the problem even before Thompson's arrival. In 1950 Harwood sent him to the Pacific Coast on a fact-finding tour, and his report of conversations with brokers, assureds, the Board of Marine Underwriters of San Francisco, and individual surveyors resulted in Thompson's being authorized to make West Coast reorganization one of his initial targets.

It was on the Great Lakes, however, that the first new postwar exclusive office was opened. On his way to the Coast in June, 1951, the new general manager stopped over in Chicago to inspect Association arrangements at that port and was far from satisfied with what he found. Launched in the thirties as a branch of Cleveland, the Chicago operation had now become, in his view, so inadequate and inefficient as to require immediate inauguration of an exclusive office under a qualified lake surveyor transferred from Cleveland. Unwilling to defer the matter even until his return from California, he wrote Cornwell at once urging that the change be made by August 1. This plan was adopted by the directors on June 21.

Guy Myers now found himself directing three exclusive

offices, Buffalo, Cleveland, and Chicago, as principal surveyor
of the Great Lakes District. This situation would continue until
his retirement October 31, 1954, when he was succeeded as
principal surveyor by James C. Sherman, his assistant for the
preceding year and a quarter. Myers would remain an adviser
under contract, however, until the fall of 1956, thus rounding
out an even thirty years' service.

Conversion of the Gulf and West Coast agencies to exclusive offices under district headquarters began simultaneously
in 1952 and moved ahead on parallel courses through Thompson's first five years. Both were large projects requiring broad
diplomatic preparation and intensive organizational planning.

Since before the war, Association representation in both
the East and West Gulf had been contracted to William Freeman as agent. One of the Association's original employees,
having started in Syndicate "A's" old New Orleans branch,
Freeman now maintained his own offices both there and in

Righting operations in progress on the capsized *American Tidelands Drilling Rig
101* in the Gulf of Mexico, 1955: one of the Association's early contacts with the
offshore drilling industry.

Houston. Thompson's aim was to establish exclusive Association offices in each port. To clear the way in a "fair and equitable" manner, it was voted April 17, 1952, to buy out Freeman's agency contract on terms which guaranteed him three years' salary as an adviser, provided that during that time he should "not engage in any marine activities either directly or indirectly" without written approval.

This agreement concluded, the establishment of the new offices moved forward. Houston was opened under the Association name on July 1, 1952; New Orleans, on March 1, 1953. Freeman's premises were taken over, with those of his staff who chose to stay on, and for the first time in many years the Association was handling its own business in Gulf waters.

Present at the opening of both new offices was a recent addition to the surveying staff who was to figure importantly in the Association's future. John R. Lindgren was one of the "war generation" of younger men which came into the organization near the time of Thompson's appointment, progressively relieving the veterans of the formative decades, and lending power to the reorganization drive. Hired in New York in March, 1952, at the age of 44, he was assigned six months' temporary duty at Houston, then transferred to New Orleans as resident surveyor to open the office there. In April, 1956, the whole coast from Texas to Florida was brought under his aegis as principal surveyor of the Gulf area, and in the same year the number of offices in the area was doubled, with the opening of exclusive facilities at Mobile, Alabama, on May 1 and at Beaumont, Texas, on September 1.

Meanwhile, in the West, even more sweeping changes were in progress. Cornwell's 1950 survey and two 1951 trips by Thompson satisfied the Association that it was time to supersede the quarter-century-old arrangement with the San Francisco Board. That body acquiesced at a meeting attended by Thompson, November 6, 1951, and the Association voted nine days later to go ahead.

But going ahead meant dealing with problems of a complexity and delicacy not present in the Gulf situation. As in 1930 on the Lakes, the Association was now invading an area where regional customs and loyalties were strong, and doing so virtually as a newcomer. True, it had for years been represented by the Board. But since Young's death in 1938, and McAlinden's unsuccessful effort to recruit as his successor Walter Martignoni, West Coast surveyor famed for the 1930 *Tamiahua* salvage, no one had borne the title of principal surveyor for the United States Salvage Association on that coast. If its services were to be drawn upon by anyone other than Syndicate members (and even they were by no means unanimous in their support), there was a major public relations job to be done.

It became clear that the westward move would have to be taken in steps. San Francisco was a big enough initial project without simultaneously taking over the Board's offices in other Pacific ports, particularly in view of certain knotty organizational and financial problems, chiefly the apportionment of responsibility for funding pensions of employees who had served the Board for years but would retire as Association hull surveyors. Despite strong cooperation by the Board and its secretary Jack Waddington, it was over two years before these obstacles were cleared. By then the Board had also disposed of its cargo-surveying activities, to the newly-formed National Cargo Bureau.

To reestablish an Association office in San Francisco, Pulliam was sent west in 1952, with the title of Pacific Coast manager. (His former title of technical assistant in New York was subsequently borne by Sherman before his own transfer to Cleveland.) On May 1 the new office assumed direct responsibility for the San Francisco area, the Board continuing to represent the Association elsewhere.

Not until over two years later, on October 1, 1954, did the Association formally absorb all hull-surveying activities of the San Francisco Board. This added three new exclusive offices in United States ports: Los Angeles (Wilmington), California; Portland, Oregon; and Seattle, Washington. It made Pulliam, in effect, the principal surveyor of a coast district, though he retained the title of manager until his retirement in 1962.

A Pacific comber explodes against the side of the doomed *Chickasaw* at Santa Rosa Island, California, in February, 1962, as Devine's *Salvage Chief* unloads cargo by high line into a barge anchored between them (see p. 157).

A third California office, San Diego, was added in October, 1956. Both the then-territories of Hawaii and Alaska were also encompassed in Pulliam's area. The agency at Honolulu (where the Association was represented by the American Bureau of Shipping) came under San Francisco's jurisdiction in 1952 and was replaced by an exclusive office May 1, 1961; but, despite moves at the same period "to put a man in Alaska," Thompson decided not to disturb the existing jurisdiction of the Pacific District (normally exercised through the Seattle office), which continues today.

To smooth the transition and foster local use of Association services, the San Francisco Board agreed to the appointment of its entire board of directors as the Association's Pacific Coast Advisory Committee. That there were real grounds for worry on this score was demonstrated in 1958, when lack of native underwriter support forced the closing of the two-year-old San Diego office. Despite such setbacks, however, there were steady gains in most ports, as local confidence was won, and by early 1962 the chairman of the Advisory Committee could report a "gratifying . . . acceptance of the Association," which, he said, "all in all, . . . had gained in stature" along the Pacific seaboard.

Prior to 1954, Canadian West Coast ports had come within the scope of the San Francisco Board agency, through an office headed by Captain Frederick L. Clarke in Vancouver, British Columbia. It was planned to include this office in the general transfer of authority, but discussions during 1953 disclosed some Canadian coolness toward working in an office which had "United States" as part of its name. In the general shift of 1954, therefore, a new "division" of the Association came into being under the name Marine Surveyors of Western Canada, with Clarke as division manager. This arrangement has worked well to this day, and recently, with the significant increase in Arctic assignments, the Marine Surveyors have come to handle all jobs on the Canadian side of the line, as the Association's Seattle office does those on the Alaskan.

Back on the East Coast, regional reorganization had lagged somewhat behind the more critical Gulf and Pacific areas. Thompson's plans, however, recognized Atlantic "blank spots," and gradually four more exclusive offices joined the list: Jacksonville (1955), Miami (1958), Baltimore (1959), and Philadelphia (1962). Two of these, Jacksonville and Philadelphia, had been among the earliest ports served by Syndicate "A," but had been shut down since 1921.

Cornwell and Thompson did not intend that this broad increase in direct Association field capacity should stop at the continental limits. We have already seen how the former laid the groundwork, as far back as 1949, for converting the General European Agency into an exclusive London office. With this plan in view, Edward Ganly, who had first gone to London as a 22-year-old Webb Institute graduate in 1937 to assist Alden, was sent again as an Association employee in 1949 after six years in New York and three in the Navy. On November 1,

1953, the day after Alden's retirement, he was installed in the Association's first office on foreign soil, as principal surveyor in charge for Europe.

This title meant that Ganly, like Alden, would have general jurisdiction over all ports in Europe and throughout the Mediterranean area. Though Thompson had suggested in 1953 that "direct control" in the latter area would be improved by a separate office "possibly in Genoa," this was never followed up. The passage of a few years did, however, confirm Cornwell's 1949 forecast that expansion of northwestern Europe's ports and shipyards would soon require a continental office. London was still retained as overall headquarters, but in 1961 an exclusive office was opened in Rotterdam, replacing the former Amsterdam and Rotterdam representatives. Edward F. Brough, formerly of John Mitchell's Baltimore office, was sent over as resident surveyor.

Serious thought was also given to direct representation in the Far East, where the Association had always worked through agents and where, Thompson reported in December, 1954, "supervision is not good." He considered an office advisable at Kobe, Japan, and said definite recommendations might be forthcoming in six months; but it was to be almost nine years before existing arrangements in Asia were disturbed.

One other full-fledged foreign office was, however, established in the fifties as an adjunct to American ore and oil activities—particularly the latter—in Venezuela. Late in 1954 it was found necessary to appoint a local representative to deal with the ore carriers plying out of the Orinoco, and four years later an oil-drilling rush in the Maracaibo area brought into being at that port the Association's first exclusive office in South America. It was opened March 1, 1959, with Edward M. Brady, from the recently closed San Diego office, as resident surveyor. So strenuous was the pace that before the end of the year a second surveyor had to be assigned.

The drilling and pipeline boom passed quickly, however. By 1961 it was possible to cut the office back to one surveyor, and by the end of 1964 most American-insured equipment had finished its work and moved elsewhere. Shipping persisted, but not in a volume to justify the upkeep of a full office. Hence, on October 31, 1965, Maracaibo followed San Diego into history, and the Venezuelan area reverted to local representation.

It could no longer be called agency representation. Always sensitive, by the very nature of its work, to potential liability for improper or unauthorized conduct of those who acted in its behalf, the Association had taken various steps on advice of counsel, in 1953-1954, "to reduce such exposure to a minimum." One of these was the cancellation on March 1, 1954, of all agents' appointments throughout the world, followed by redesignation of the same individuals and firms as "representatives," the title which remains in use today.

⚓ ⚓ ⚓

By the end of 1961, when Thompson's policies had been actually operative for only a few months over a decade, those policies had so altered the Association in size, form, and func-

Like a gargantuan flower arrangement, convoluted hull plating of the *Del Mar* frames the unfinished Mississippi River bridge at New Orleans. This damage, caused by striking a dock in 1957, was of a sort highlighted in the Association's cargo ship damage study six years later (see p. 174).

tion as to have strained the credulity of a John Rohde, let alone a David Young or a Lawrence Brengle, had they returned for an inspection. To cite only a few dimensional consequences of the Organization Program, the number of exclusive offices throughout the world (excluding San Diego, which had closed, and Philadelphia, which had not yet opened) now totaled 22, a 450% increase over the 4 of 1950. Surveying and technical staff had increased proportionately, from 13 to 70. Clerical staff was up from 19 to 63.

Fully as impressive were the gains in income and survey volume. The stockholders were told at their 1962 annual meeting that 14,277 surveys had been attended in the previous year, a 137% increase over 1950. Gross income was $1,973,591, a 318% increase. Despite enlargement of payroll and other costs, it had proved possible to accomplish the Pacific Coast takeover in 1954 without recourse to stockholder assessment, and things were in good enough shape by 1957, it will be recalled, to permit retirement of all the 5% preferred stock, only three years after it was issued.

In another matter, close to the hearts of Association leaders for decades, the events of the fifties were yielding most encouraging results. This was heightened stockholder use of the organization's facilities and an even more significant increase in work performed for nonsyndicate members and nonunderwriters. Between 1950 and 1954 the share of total billings chargeable to the Hull and Great Lakes Syndicates dropped from 61.4% to 44.8%; the share of surveys, from 57.6% to 35.5%. A tabular breakdown of business by sources covering the years 1958-1961, inclusive, showed all syndicate business falling from 44.8% to 36.9%, member company (i.e., stockholder) patronage holding almost exactly even, and work for all "others" rising from 36.3% to 44.3%.

The "others" included "outside" underwriters, American and foreign, and a considerable clientele entirely beyond the insurance pale. In the early fifties misgivings were still felt as to how far and on what terms the Association should serve outsiders. It took three months in 1953 to decide, in connection with a request by Gough & King "as binding agents for the

Saskatchewan Government Insurance Office," that "the function of the Salvage Association is to provide survey services to commercial underwriting organizations to the extent that this proves practicable." Four years later, survey requests by the Dowa Fire & Marine Insurance Company and the Ultramar Inter-America Corporation elicited the view "that the Salvage Association should not provide such services on an agency basis but . . . on a case-by-case basis"—with advance assurance of payment! In March, 1959, arrangements were announced with the Comité Central des Assureurs Maritimes de France to attend surveys for French underwriters in the continental United States.

The most noteworthy class of new business developed during this period of expansion was for a customer which had not—except in wartime—made any significant call on Association facilities since 1931, the United States Government. As the decade advanced, the Maritime Administration and other federal agencies sought advice and assistance on a number of programs which, in variety and sophistication, dwarfed the condition and damage surveys of the twenties. The more important and interesting of these contract projects will be described in the chapters to follow.

All these things reflected the remarkable gains in maturity, scope, and professional standing which the United States Salvage Association had achieved in a decade of strenuous reprogramming. One more step remained to be taken in the fifties, signifying and solidifying these gains. At the annual meeting in 1958, it was voted to recast the titles of the three highest offices, thus representing more appropriately the current function of each. The former presidency and vice presidency were redesignated the chairmanship and vice chairmanship of the board, and Clifford G. Cornwell and Harold Jackson were named to these new positions, respectively. The general managership was concurrently abolished and replaced by a new presidency, to which J. Paul Thompson was elected. The Association thus attained what would be its command format for the balance of its first half-century.

XV

SAVANNAH, SATURN, AND THE
SUBSIDIZED LINES

THE adage that business flows to the door of a busy man applies as well to organizations as to individuals. For the Association, the expansive fifties were marked not only by burgeoning survey work but by a growing number of study and advisory programs for governmental or quasi-governmental clients. We have seen how the first of these, the Navy "JAG" agreement, grew out of wartime service to that federal department. The second, a series of foreign repair cost studies for the Maritime Administration and the subsidized steamship lines, was undertaken simultaneously with the Organization Program.

For fifteen years after the Merchant Marine Act of 1936 established U.S.-foreign cost differentials as the basis of public financial encouragement to American-flag shipping, abnormal world conditions hampered development of procedures for determining these differentials. Immediate postwar efforts resulted in duplicative and to some extent conflicting findings by public agencies and private ship operators as to foreign repair cost levels. An unfortunate side-effect of this activity was that overseas shipyards wearied of furnishing the same data to two or more groups of American investigators. In fact, Alden reported from London in 1950 that Britain's influential Shipbuilding Conference had lost patience and ruled that its members need no longer respond to such inquiries.

This threatened roadblock to national maritime policy impelled the Government and private steamship operators to seek an impartial, technically qualified third party to ascertain and report foreign repair yard costs, as an essential ingredient in calculating "operating-differential subsidy." Their decision was to approach the United States Salvage Association.

DISINTEGRATION
ON THE DELAWARE

Early in March, 1957, the MSTS tanker *Mission San Francisco* was in collision on the Delaware with the freighter *Elna II*. In ballast and not gas-freed, the big ship literally disintegrated, leaving only the extreme bow and stern intact and heaping the channel bottom with tons of jumbled steel. As this was brought to the surface and collected at the Philadelphia Navy Yard, Association surveyor Harry Townsend was called in to spend days sorting and identifying it. His marks appear on the pieces pictured here (see p. 176).

4th Naval District photos

The initial overture was a telephone call to Cornwell from Frank A. Nemec of New Orleans in August, 1950. Nemec, secretary-treasurer of Lykes Bros. Steamship Co., was speaking for the thirteen liner companies which then held operating-differential subsidy contracts with the Maritime Administration. Although Cornwell, as yet, held no Association office, he was already designated to succeed Harwood in the presidency. In subsequent correspondence he expressed willingness to explore the use of the Association's overseas organization in collecting the desired data if the plan had the backing of the Maritime Administration "and others concerned." This set the stage for almost ten months' negotiation of specifics.

The "others concerned" were chiefly the General Accounting Office, whose concurrence was required in all aspects of subsidy determination. Upon being advised, through Nemec, that this clearance had been received, along with Maritime Administration approval of the general concept, the Management Committee on November 22 agreed to examine "the full scope and conditions of the task," a project in which Thompson assumed a leading role upon becoming general manager. In a letter of May 9, 1951, to the Maritime Administration, he set forth the guidelines which would govern this and succeeding studies.

These provided that Association representatives abroad would receive estimates furnished by their local ship repairers in response to a standard form of inquiry, and transmit them to New York with an indication whether or not they were reasonably in line with current practice. After consolidation at New York they would be transmitted as confidential information to the Office of Subsidy and Government Aid in Washington. By a separate contract, the subsidized lines undertook to pay all costs of the program; but the Association's service obligation was to the Maritime Administration, whose Deputy Administrator, Earl W. Clark, set the first study in motion by a formal letter of request and agreement June 7, 1951.

This initial project was something of a trial run for all parties, and special effort was exerted to make it successful, McAlinden being dispatched to oversee its inauguration in the

European and African areas. Requests were directed to 106 yards throughout the world, 92 of which responded with estimates reflecting 1951 repair cost levels. These were processed and in government hands by mid-April, 1952. By May the steamship lines' committee had expressed formal satisfaction with the result.

Since this propitious start, the Association has been recurrently commissioned to perform world-wide surveys for Maritime Administration use at approximate three-year intervals: specifically for the years 1953, 1956, 1959, 1963, 1966, and 1969. The range of coverage was steadily broadened and deepened down to 1963, when 188 yards were queried, though only 80% of them responded. Costs of the second through the sixth survey were borne by the Committee of American Steamship Lines ("CASL"), organized in 1953 to represent various common interests of subsidized American-flag operators, the program's chief beneficiaries. By 1969, CASL had merged with the American Merchant Marine Institute and the Pacific American Steamship Association to form the American Institute of Merchant Shipping ("AIMS"). This organization underwrote the 1969 study, which will be the last under the 1936 Act, since, by the time it was completed, the Merchant Marine Act of 1970 had replaced the earlier statute.

⚓   ⚓   ⚓

Six years after the first repair cost study, the Maritime Administration turned to the Association with a new contract proposal. Now the federal agency was involved, jointly with the Atomic Energy Commission, in implementing the Government's most forward-looking maritime program: the introduction of nuclear propulsion to world merchant shipping. With the Nuclear Ship *Savannah* already on order, a wide range of data had to be assembled looking toward her future commercial operation. Out of this need arose the Nuclear Hazards Program, and a new sphere of usefulness for the Association.

Ever since the war's end, there had been lively interest throughout the engineering profession in the peacetime potential of atomic power. Since the commissioning of the first nu-

When the *Savannah*, world's first nuclear merchant ship, was new, this model of her was pictured along with one (roughly to scale) of her namesake, the pioneer transatlantic steamer of 1819. Holding the latter is actress Mary Fickett, a direct descendant of the original *Savannah's* builder.

Author's collection

clear warship, the United States submarine *Nautilus,* in 1954, marine engineers in particular had sought all available information on the applicability of the new power source to merchant shipping. Thompson reported in 1955, "Your Association is a member of the Atomic Industrial Forum and is endeavoring to keep abreast of development in the nuclear power field, including all types of power-producing units." As government planning in this field progressed, the Association was granted an Atomic Energy Commission "Access Permit" on April 24, 1957, followed by clearance for storage of classified documents. During the same year six staff members received personal "QX" security clearance from the AEC.

It was therefore natural that, when faced with the need to develop safety criteria for incorporation in the *Savannah's* construction, the Government should turn to the Association as one of the organizations best qualified to collect and interpret such data. On January 27, 1958, it let a contract under which the Association became responsible for the second phase of a four-phase program to define and, so far as possible, to counter in advance the safety hazards to which nuclear merchantmen would be exposed. Watkins, then the Association's chief engineer, was placed in charge. The other contractors were the Arthur D. Little Corporation (Phase 1) and Gibbs & Cox, Inc. (Phases 3 and 4).

It was the function of Phases 1 and 2 to collect and organize data for study and planning use in Phases 3 and 4. Phase 1, concerning safety aspects of atomic power application, was largely theoretical, since the application was now being made, to merchant ships, for the first time. Phase 2, on the contrary, was intensely factual and enormously detailed. It involved collecting and analyzing data on hundreds of accidents to *conventionally powered* merchant ships during 1953-1956, inclusive. By sorting over this massive record, it was hoped to establish statistical trends as to the causes and consequences of various types of casualty, the probability and severity of damage under given conditions, dominant forms of structural injury, areas of greatest vulnerability, etc.

In the context of 1971, when many years' safe operation by the *Savannah* and other ships has shown nuclear power to be not noticeably more hazardous than other forms of power associated with shipping, these precautionary studies may seem overelaborate and even hysterical. It is already hard to remember with what deep apprehension many, even among educated people, viewed the adaptation of atomic power to peaceful uses in the late fifties. The United States Government, well aware that its Atoms for Peace program would be eyed even more warily abroad, was determined to spare no effort to make the *Savannah* the safest vessel afloat. To this end, the Association's part in the Nuclear Hazards Program was indispensable and well worthwhile.

The completion and official acceptance of this study, reported by Thompson at the 1959 annual meeting, was by no means the end of Association interest in the *Savannah* program or in nuclear technology generally. Already, in 1958, a staff member had been put through the sixth-month training course then being offered at the Babcock & Wilcox Nuclear Facility in Lynchburg, Virginia, as an adjunct to the atomic ship project.

In addition to following closely the construction, launching, trials, and operation of the *Savannah,* the Association supported nuclear development in 1959 by contributing to the Special Nuclear Fund of the American Standards Association. Later that year and early in 1960 it also contributed to shaping international nuclear agreements, being represented at all meetings of the Nuclear Power Committee to determine the United States position for revision of the International Safety of Life at Sea Convention, 1948. Despite the apparent slackening of American interest in nuclear marine propulsion development in recent years, which threatens at this writing to surrender to other nations our early leadership in this field, the Association remains in a position to lend technical support to any renewal of the program.

⚓   ⚓   ⚓

If the work of the Association figuratively soared to new heights in the fifties, it quite literally went into orbit in the sixties, when its surveyors and technicians made an inconspicuous but vital contribution to the vast complex of coordinated effort which placed the first men on the moon. The logistic dilemma which made humanity's newest mode of long-distance travel momentarily dependent upon its oldest is an intriguing quirk of the space age.

By 1960 rocket engines, though capable of transporting men at dizzy speeds above the earth, had attained such massive proportions that men were hard-pressed to transport *them* on its surface. The first "Saturns" for the Apollo Program—burly cylinders 85 feet long by 27 in diameter—were being built for the National Aeronautics and Space Administration ("NASA") in Huntsville, Alabama, at the George C. Marshall Space Flight Center. This placed them some 550 miles from their Florida launching platform, as the rocket flies. But the Saturns could not fly until they reached Cape Canaveral, then so called, nor could they travel by any existing road or railway. There remained the water route, a route which started in precisely the wrong direction—toward Tennessee—and snaked through 2,250 miles of river and ocean.

What was demanded was a sustained towage program of unusual intricacy and abnormal risk. For the organization, approval, and supervision of such a program during the coming decade, NASA turned to the United States Salvage Association.

The contract between them, effective December 18, 1960, provided for a much broader area of responsibility than mere arranging of a single tow or series of tows. Its central provision was that the Association was to "examine and make recommendations for any NASA craft to be made fit for being towed to a specific destination in either inland waters or between points on the United States coasts." It was to do likewise with all towing vessels proposed to be used, and all towing gear and equipment. Not until it was satisfied by subsequent inspection that the Government and contractors involved had complied with its recommendations was its approval to be given. It was to have similar power of approval over handling and stowage, "towing method and hook-up," and routing.

Nor did the Association's responsibility end with the preparatory phases. It was to evaluate all damage from marine casualties involving NASA vessels, and to perform "surveys, marine or otherwise," on any "marine craft, structures, or ships" concerned in the agency's missions. Finally, leaving no doubt that this was a comprehensive agreement for professional counsel, the contract directed generally that the Association "perform advisory services to Government when technical marine knowledge is required."

A specialized barge, the *Palaemon,* already constructed to carry the booster, was examined and approved by the Association early in 1961. It was the prototype of a series of such carriers, fitted with air-conditioned "Quonset"-style deckhouses to protect their huge but delicate cargo against climatic changes on a trip through ten degrees of latitude and twelve of longitude. After local trials on the Tennessee River, a complete "dummy" run was made from Huntsville to Cape Canaveral under Association surveillance.

The barge *Palaemon,* incorporating Association suggestions and inspected under
the initial NASA-USSA contract in 1961.

S-IC-10 booster engine, of the type used for the Apollo XV shot in 1971, being
loaded on the barge *Poseidon.*

Photos courtesy National Aeronautics & Space Administration

In the fall of 1961, about the time when the first actual booster shipment was under way, word was received that security clearances would be required for Association personnel in the future. This, it developed, was occasioned by the need of their counsel in connection with transporting the far larger rocket engines then under classified development. Matters were stalled for some months by Department of Defense objections to the partly foreign ownership of the Association's stock (about 18½% being then held by admitted companies), but the difficulty was finally resolved and the clearances issued September 26, 1962.

During the following years, towage approval was by no means the only service rendered under the contract. In 1962-1963, for example, a study was made of self-propelled seagoing vessels capable of carrying space vehicles, with reference both to convertibility of existing tonnage and to new construction. But, throughout, a steady succession of Saturns moved toward Florida, either from Huntsville or from NASA facilities near New Orleans. The operation, and the hardware, grew in size and sophistication, right down to the mighty engine that tossed Apollo XV into space. By contrast with the 85-foot booster of only seven years before, Saturn V, shipped from New Orleans in 1968 on the barge *Poseidon* to send the men of Apollo VIII around the moon for the first time, measured 138 x 35 feet.

The day-to-day conduct of the NASA program, whether Huntsville or New Orleans was the shipping point, devolved on the Association's New Orleans office, headed until 1967 by Joseph K. Tynan, and thereafter by James F. Kanapaux. Their contribution, and that of the entire Association, to the development of manned space flight was publicly recognized after the Apollo VIII success by NASA's presentation to Kanapaux and New Orleans Surveyors Peter S. Odin, Sheldon G. Held, and John C. Long of commemorative medals cast in part from a piece of aluminum which had been carried around the moon. The letter of presentation said, "This medallion is given . . . to show to each of you our sincere appreciation for your outstanding efforts that have helped to make our previous flights a successful reality, as well as for the missions that remain ahead."

NATIONAL AERONAUTICS AND SPACE ADMINISTRATION
GEORGE C. MARSHALL SPACE FLIGHT CENTER
MARSHALL SPACE FLIGHT CENTER, ALABAMA 35812

September 9, 1969

IN REPLY REFER TO:

Mr. James F. Kanapaux
Principal Surveyor
Gulf District
U.S. Salvage Association
226 Carondelet Street
New Orleans, La. 70130

Dear Mr. Kanapaux:

As so many people have worked in our transportation effort to make manned space flight possible, it seemed to me that there should be some way of providing those who worked in the space program some symbol of their efforts.

The first manned lunar flight, Apollo 8, carried a piece of aluminum which was melted down and incorporated into the metal used in making this commemorative medallion. A similar medallion was carried by Astronauts Borman, Lovell and Anders during their December flight.

This medallion is given with the desire that it will bring you a sense of active participation in our manned space flight program. It is also to show to each of you our sincere appreciation for your outstanding efforts that have helped to make our previous flights a successful reality, as well as for the missions that remain ahead.

Carl D. DeNeen
Chief, Transport Branch
Project Logistics Office

Enclosure:
As stated

NASA medal and letter of commendation presented to the New Orleans surveying staff after the Apollo VIII flight.

128

XVI

CROSS-WINDS IN THE SIXTIES

T HERE had been no doubt in what direction the Association
was moving in the fifties. Every light was green, every
system "go."

As we have seen, the key statistics more than doubled under the impetus of new organization, new financing, and new
scope. Free to expand for the first time in thirty years, the Association steadily matched its growing capacity with increased
opportunities for service.

In the sixties, climatic conditions were more confused, for
the Association as for the country and the world. Momentum
was not lost—indeed, in many respects, full realization of the
objectives of the reorganization still lay ahead—but now there
were new factors to slow and complicate the almost unbroken
forward movement of the previous decade. In particular, drastic
changes were taking place in shipping, and especially in American shipping, which could not fail to affect deeply, for better
or worse, the organizations which existed to insure and to service it.

The quandary of the times is typified by the fact that
throughout the last decade the two chief statistical gauges of
organizational progress, number of surveys performed and volume of income, have moved in opposite directions. From 1960
through 1970, annual survey volume, which had reached its
all-time peak in 1957, declined by 27%, with decreases in eight
years out of the ten. Yet in the same period gross income rose
by 70%, with increases every year but one.

The paradox is of course more apparent than real. Even
allowing for inflation, it is clear that the Association has advanced financially. As for the drop in surveys, a number of
factors are involved, among them the sharp and continuing

Pioneer Muse forebody aslant on the rocks of Minami Daito Shima, October, 1961 (see p. 157). Her crumpled stern is bent back out of sight behind the deckhouse.

The only "harbor" accessible to the wreck; salvors picking their way gingerly

decrease in the American-flag merchant fleet, the general tendency to replace many small ships with fewer large ones, a period relatively free from major casualties in some areas, and the widespread inclusion of "deductibles" in hull insurance policies, resulting in a tendency to confine calls for survey to significant damage cases, and to eliminate small "nuisance" requests. Nevertheless, this is the longest single period in Association history when income and survey volume have trended apart.

A substantial offset to any shrinkage in traditional sources of business has been the consistent expansion of work for non-Syndicate clients. In the past nine years such work has increased from 44.3% of total Association business to 54.8%. The 1961 percentage was not broken down, but that for 1970 was allocated 9.5% to nonmember insurance companies, 45.3% to "others"—including brokers, vessel and equipment owners, and governmental units. On this showing, the Association is already performing over half its work for clients other than those it was created in 1921 to serve—surely remarkable evidence of growth.

Also indicative of broadening activity is the record of the annual charges paid to the Syndicate by the Association for clerical and office services received at their common business address, 99 John Street, New York City. At the depth of the Depression, it will be recalled, this fee had stood at a token $6,000; by 1935, at $12,500. But these were trifles by post-1950 standards. In 1955 the Association paid $50,000. With expansion in full swing, the charge rose above $70,000 by 1957, passing $80,000 in 1960, $90,000 in 1967, and $100,000 in 1969. In 1971 it stands at $106,000.

The years 1960-1963 brought the final reorganizational moves under Thompson's program, in New York and the field, followed by his retirement and a series of top personnel changes from which the Association emerged very much as it is constituted today. Early in 1960 John Lindgren was brought from New Orleans to the home office and named assistant to the president. This was followed by revival of the post of chief surveyor, and by creation on December 1, 1961, of three new vice presidencies, with Lindgren as vice president—chief surveyor, Watkins as vice president—operations, and Townsend as vice president—research and technical. Upon Watkins' resignation the following October, however, his office became vacant and remained so for the rest of the decade.

June, 1960, had marked the accomplishment of one other item in Thompson's 1951 plan: creation of a principal surveyorship for the Atlantic district, with jurisdiction from Maine to the Florida Capes. The initial incumbent was Ganly, who had returned from London the year before and assumed the New York area post, vacant since Henry resigned in 1958. Ganly himself resigned at the end of 1960, but the district post, now permanently established, was filled by Richard A. Cady, who two years earlier had succeeded Ganly as principal surveyor for Europe. The planned pattern of four mainland districts was completed in 1962 when Pulliam retired as Pacific Coast manager and was succeeded by Robert W. Lees, with the title principal surveyor, Pacific district.

The first of two major retirements in 1963 was that of Romer F. Weyant, treasurer of both Association and Syndicate since he succeeded Schuler in 1947. Like his predecessor, Weyant had played a very active role in the internal affairs of the organization. His place was taken by Robert T. Luehman.

Paul Thompson stepped down as president on December 31, 1963. Since he was returning to California, the Directors took the opportunity to appoint him to the Association's Pacific Coast Advisory Committee. He was saluted on his retirement as "personally responsible" for much of the Association's great development during his thirteen years at its helm and for "carrying out the wish and mandate of the Board to build an organization such as was needed to meet the international needs of the American Merchant Marine and the American Marine Insurance Market."

By singular coincidence, another Californian who had been his earliest predecessor in the management of the Association and Syndicate "A," Charles R. Page, died on the West Coast in the year of Thompson's retirement.

The sixties also saw the retirement of two veteran staff members whose combined service in the New York office to-

JOHN R. LINDGREN
Association President since 1964

talled 99 years: Frances B. Kieran and Charles J. Monaghan. The former, who had come to Syndicate "A" as a stenographer in November, 1920, almost a year before the Association was activated, retired as office supervisor October 31, 1967. "Charlie" Monaghan, who had transferred to the Association a few months after joining Syndicate "C" in December, 1925, and had been accounting clerk under three treasurers—Schuler, Weyant, and Luehman—retired five months after Miss Kieran.

At the December, 1963, meeting John R. Lindgren was named to succeed Thompson in the presidency on New Year's Day. Since January, 1963, he had served as executive vice president—chief surveyor, with authority to act for the president in

133

most matters. Harry S. Townsend was reelected vice president, an office he still holds today.

Technically, the new president's position in the chain of command was still subordinate to that of the board chairman and Syndicate manager, Clifford G. Cornwell. But Cornwell, though keenly interested in the Association and always in touch with it on the policy level, construed his own role as one of counsel and review, and continued the practice he had followed in Thompson's case: choosing a professional in whom he had confidence and leaving in his hands the direction of a professional organization. He was supported in this course through the sixties by successive vice chairmen: Robert R. Dwelly of the Insurance Company of North America, Gilbert B. Oxford of the Boston Insurance Company, Walter R. Gherardi of Chubb & Son, William R. McBean of the Washington General Insurance Company, G. Doane McCarthy of the Fireman's Fund Insurance Company, and George H. Bunyan of the Royal Insurance Company. Thus underwriter control of an organization owned by underwriters was maintained, but, under the chairman's practical and diplomatic approach, it was *remote* control, to a degree unimaginable in prewar days.

After a decade's successful operation as a business venture since abandoning the old break-even basis, the Association determined at the start of 1965 that its expanding activities would shortly require a broadened financial base. To raise its capitalization from $100,000 to $200,000, while providing a substantial reserve of treasury shares for future exigencies, it increased the authorized common stock from 2,000 to 8,000 shares and declared a 100% stock dividend to the holders of the original 2,000. A semi-annual dividend payment of $2.50 per share on the 4,000 issued shares was simultaneously established but given up two years later in favor of a policy of declaring annual dividends in amounts to be determined by the directors. This policy still prevails in the semicentennial year.

⚓ ⚓ ⚓

The dawn of that year brought to completion the Association's present leadership structure, with Cornwell's retire-

ALLEN E. SCHUMACHER
Chairman of the Association Board of Directors, 1971

ment and the succession to its chairmanship and the Syndicate's of Allen E. Schumacher. Unlike previous chairmen, Schumacher has already been closely affiliated with the Association's work for years, since joining the Syndicate Claims Department in 1955. As claims manager from 1960 to 1967, he was necessarily in daily contact with Association officers and surveyors, inasmuch as the critical first hours of major damage cases invariably require close liaison between claims men and the surveyors on whom they depend for field intelligence and technical guidance.

The new chairman has declared his intention to follow the general approach of his predecessor as far as delegation of operational authority to the president is concerned. He anticipates that his own role will be one of counsel, review, and support at the policy level. On the other hand, with his background of claims and his awareness of the important working relationship between underwriter and surveyor, it is to be expected that he will maintain a close and active interest in the affairs of the Association and in the surveyors themselves.

⚓   ⚓   ⚓

The last ten years have brought no change in the lineup of Association offices around the North American coastline, including Hawaii. The slow general decline in survey volume has affected different offices in varying degree at various times but has tended, on the whole, to average out. For instance, although recurrent concern had been expressed over an apparent falling off of large-vessel business at Baltimore, that office was one of only six which did *not* show a decline in survey activity for 1970. Reasons cited for sagging business at different times and places included several prolonged shipping strikes, the apparently permanent layup of all American-flag passenger liners on the East Coast, the emphasis on "deductibles" already mentioned, and inflation of operating costs, with a consequent need for higher fees.

It is such conditions, coupled with fundamental changes in what might be called the master patterns of shipping, which tend to bring chronic organizational problems into focus. The question arises, on the one hand, whether the business available to a particular existing office has diminished to the point where it would be more economical to service it at long range from another office than to retain present facilities. On the other hand, have patterns so changed in a given remote area as to make it more efficient to set up an office there than to continue long-distance attendance of surveyors from an existing office? Each of these questions has confronted the Association at least twice in the past ten years. Boston and Honolulu, through no fault of their own, find themselves in the first category, on the basis of survey volume. Yet each retains undeniable strategic value, geographically speaking. Meanwhile, shipping and other marine activities in Alaska and Puerto Rico have so expanded of late that it may soon become impracticable to service them, respectively, through Seattle and New York, as at present. At the Association's fiftieth birthday, these remain open questions; but some or all seem likely to be early agenda items in the second half-century.

The Pacific area, on the whole, fared better in the sixties than others. In March, 1966, Fred W. Galbreath, chairman of the Pacific Coast Committee, reported to the directors that recent months "had produced the greatest increase in business in many years on the Pacific Coast, particularly in the San Francisco area." A prominent contributing cause was, of course, the great expansion in transpacific American shipping as a result of the Vietnamese War. This, together with accelerated maritime activity arising from Alaskan and Hawaiian statehood, undoubtedly contributed strongly to consolidating the Association's recently established independent operation on the Coast. Conversely, the sharp decrease of shipping to Southeast Asia in 1969 and 1970 operated to bring Pacific volume back into line with the depressed conditions obtaining in the other coast districts.

The remaining domestic area, the Great Lakes, was the only one to undergo major change in the sixties: two major changes, in fact. The first, which actually occurred on the eve of the new decade but had an impact which has not yet subsided, was the opening of the St. Lawrence Seaway. This is not the place to assess the full economic and technological consequences of that historic event, but certain direct and indirect effects on Association operations are at once apparent. The patterns of both the grain and ore trades were substantially altered. What had been a trickle of miniscule ocean tonnage became a major influx of international shipping, accustomed to navigating under rules appreciably at variance with those prevailing on the Lakes. And the establishment of a new "main line" undermined the business and prestige of the historic terminal port of Buffalo, New York.

In a multitude of ways, these changes altered and augmented the problems of insurers and surveyors on the Lakes. Collisions, groundings, and other accidents multiplied and, to

THE SEAWAY WAS NOT AN UNMIXED BLESSING

New "Seaway-size" Canadian carrier *Lawrencecliffe Hall* lies on her side in her namesake river after colliding with the *Sunek*, November 16, 1965. Snow already covers the shore. There would be much more, and heavy ice, before salvage was concluded.

the extent that they involved underwriters or owners who relied on Association services, expanded its duties. Such traditional Association activities as grain cargo surveys and winter moorings at Buffalo were also affected. Two major collisions of the mid-sixties happened to lake bulk carriers which would not have been where they were, meeting the ships with which they collided, but for the Seaway: the ore-laden *Lawrencecliffe Hall*, less than six months old, which rolled over in the St. Lawrence below Quebec in 1965, with winter coming on, and the *Stonefax*, which sank in the Welland Canal the next year with a cargo of fertilizer which it was feared might cause disastrous pollution. Their prolonged and difficult salvage was attended by the Association, in the former case through Hayes, Stuart, the Montreal representative; in the latter, directly by the Cleveland office under Sherman.

The second major change was internal. Early in 1968 Sherman and Elmer J. Newberry, resident surveyor at Buffalo for a decade, resigned to establish their own surveying company in a Cleveland suburb. Such resignations were by no means without precedent, as this history has shown. In fact, it has been suggested that the Association has the distinction, which is also its misfortune, of serving as the nation's chief postgraduate training school for marine surveyors, men who, when they have attained prominence in their profession, may quite understandably come to the decision that there is less future in an organization with obviously limited room at the top than in private consulting work. It thus generates its own competition, which, in the impersonal rough-and-tumble of the typical seaport, can be taken in stride. New men fill the vacancies and the work goes on. In this case Richard D. Jaeschke was promptly sent to Cleveland as principal surveyor, and David R. Downs to Buffalo.

What made this Great Lakes situation different, and more challenging for the Association, was a combination of factors, some fortuitous and some inherent in economic and social geography. Two resignees in partnership obviously posed a considerably more than doubled competitive threat, especially in a region which has always prided itself on conducting business in terms of personal reliance and loyalty—as Myers knew and Gatewood learned almost forty years earlier. Secondly, marine business at Buffalo, so hard-hit by the Seaway that the Association office there had already been cut back from two surveyors to one, offered dim prospects of supporting an increased number of American survey organizations, let alone the still highly competitive Salvage Association of London. Thirdly, the Seaway's failure to attract American-flag ocean shipping in significant volume meant that there had been little enlargement of the fleet on which American insurers were likely to request surveys. And, fourthly, by a chance which no one could in good conscience deplore, this Lake schism coincided with an extended period of almost complete freedom from major marine casualties in the area.

Organizational consequences, to this writing, have been

twofold. By late 1968 it was clear that the Buffalo office could no longer pay its way, and it was closed December 31. The establishment of a new branch office in Toledo, Ohio, planned in 1969 to cope with growing survey demand on western Lake Erie, was postponed early in 1970.

Clarification of the somewhat clouded situation in the area will depend partly on future trends in Lake/Seaway casualty volume, partly on the value local shipping interests place not merely upon the Association's emergency services but upon its unique research and technical facilities with all their implications for improved design, preventive maintenance, and safety of operation. Probably above all, it will depend on the extent to which the Association's owners utilize its facilities. It may be understandable that the Great Lakes Protective Association, after thirty years' dependence on United States Salvage Association facilities, should now have given its members an option between survey organizations; but it would be, to say the least, surprising if the underwriter proprietors found it other than advantageous to heed the president's recent appeal for their "support in using the services of this Association."

Meanwhile, Great Lakes operations are being conducted through two offices only: Cleveland and Chicago.

No additional branch facilities have been found necessary in Europe since the opening of the Rotterdam office in 1961. Lindgren, reporting as vice president—chief surveyor the next year, repeated Thompson's earlier suggestion that an exclusive office in Italy might "better serve the requirements of this area"; but the idea has not been pursued, largely because of the fortunate circumstance that the Association enjoys excellent representation at both ends of the country: Dr. Mario Galliano in Genoa and the firm of Giovanni and Ettore Sconzo in Palermo.

In 1966, as president, Lindgren reverted to the question of overseas representation, suggesting that over the past 45 years the Directory of Representatives, then standing at 110, had accumulated a substantial amount of deadwood. Being "of the firm opinion that the representative that cannot perform a proper service to us should be dropped" and "that to continue using people that we cannot fully depend on places us in a very hazardous position," he asked board authorization to prune the list in line with these principles. This was granted and, in the event, the 110 representatives were reduced to 86. In the process, attention focussed on the numerous individuals and firms who had served the Association as agents or representatives throughout its existence. In such a history as this, it is appropriate to list these overseas colleagues of a full half-century's standing:

American Trading & Shipping Co., Pty., Ltd.	Sydney, Australia
Best & Co. (Private) Ltd.	Madras, India
Blackett & Co. Ltd.	Oporto, Portugal
Donnelly & Co., S. A.	Mollendo, Peru
Peter Thr. Duborgh	Oslo, Norway
Everett Steamship Corporation	Kobe, Japan
Furness, Withy & Co., Ltd.	St. John's, Newfoundland
Gardiner Austin & Co., Ltd.	Bridgetown, Barbados
O. F. Gollcher & Sons	Valetta, Malta
Grell & Co., Ltd.	Port of Spain, Trinidad
F. E. Hardcastle & Co. (Private) Ltd.	Bombay, India
MacAndrews & Co., Ltd.	Malaga, Spain
Daniel MacPherson & Co., Ltd.	Cadiz, Spain
F. B. O'Grady & Cia. S. A.	Buenos Aires, Argentina
Modesto Pineiro y Cia.	Santander, Spain

It would be unfair to omit one other representative which wound up its foreign business just before filling out a half-century's service: the firm of Wessel, Duval & Co., Association representative in Chile and Peru from 1921 to December 10, 1970.

The latest foreign area to attain exclusive office status is the Far East. Gatewood envisioned such a development, his correspondence reveals, as early as 1930. Thompson urged it in 1954. But not until the final year of the latter's presidency was the time ripe. Part of the reason was that, as in Italy, the Association was especially fortunate in its area representative, the Everett Steamship Corporation, with "a vast network of offices in the Far East." Everett had been the intermediary in arranging surveyor attendance at the *President Hoover* stranding and most other casualties between Hokkaido and Singapore. Recently, however, it had been found necessary in cases of major

The tanker *Black Point* after a wild Pacific storm stove in both sides of her bow, necessitating emergency attendance in the Philippines and a tow to Hong Kong.

damage to send surveyors across the ocean from the Pacific District. Two such cases in 1962, the *Julesburg* and the *Black Point,* the latter involving towage from Manila to Hong Kong, were among some 300 surveys held in the Far East that year, and may have helped crystallize the decision to open an office in Japan.

Though Kobe had been first proposed as a site, and Thompson had reported after his 1962 trip that 60% of all Japanese work was performed in the Kobe/Osaka area as against 40% in the Tokyo/Yokohama area, the new office was finally located in Yokohama's Everett Building, in part for convenient access to Everett's far-flung communications system. The inaugural date was July 1, 1963, and Ralph G. Whitelaw was designated principal surveyor of the Far East District.

Whitelaw's enormous jurisdiction was divided into three sections: (1) the Japanese islands east of a north-south line midway between Yokohama and Kobe, (2) the rest of Japan, (3) the Philippines and the rest of Asia to and including Pakistan. Surveys in (1) were the direct responsibility of the district office; those in (2) were to be assigned from that office to "our representative in that area"—Everett, which usually called on the Kobe office of the American Bureau of Shipping for surveys; and those in (3) "as heretofore with our representatives," but with assignment controlled in Yokohama rather than New York or San Francisco.

Early in 1966 Lindgren visited the Far East District and returned convinced that the Yokohama staff should be expanded, so as to take over most of the Kobe area surveys. This recommendation was implemented in 1967, under a policy of employing native surveying talent in foreign offices. The appointment of J. H. W. Van Aalst at Rotterdam in 1963 was the first result of this policy (though Van Aalst had been a United States citizen for some years). It was followed the next year by the employment of Yuan Chen as the first of several Asian surveyors at Yokohama.

⚓ ⚓ ⚓

The Association's concern for the well-being of its retired employees antedates by years the general introduction of "welfare plans" in industry. As far back as 1939, it introduced a contributory plan, which was revised over the years until it became, on January 1, 1964, a fully-funded program which, as amended, compares very favorably with most programs available in industry today. The spirit motivating it was embodied in Thompson's statement to the 1956 annual meeting: "A key factor in any successful operation is the . . . performance by its staff. The significant contributions of the men and women of the Association have played no small part in our progress."

All Association employees with twenty years' service are now entitled to four-week vacations. Benefits are geared directly to income level and living standards in the years immediately preceding retirement. To give some protection against the effects of inflation, up to half of an employee's pension may, at his option, be paid as a variable annuity. Generous medical and hospital coverage, partly funded by the employee himself, and "major medical" protection, fully funded by the Association, are also included. After retirement he receives these coverages, integrated with Medicare, at no further cost to himself.

Free life insurance coverage equal to the employee's annual salary is afforded by the group insurance program, with coverage reduced after retirement. An optional survivor income program, not found in many benefit plans, is also made available, and partially paid for, by the Association, to enlarge the basic life coverage. Under its terms the employee's beneficiary will receive a regular monthly income of one-fourth his rate of earnings at the time of his death. Such benefits are guaranteed for ten years. After that period, if the beneficiary is the employee's wife, these benefits will continue until her death or remarriage —reduced by any widow's benefits due her under social security.

Noncontributory business travel accident insurance is also carried for all full-time salaried employees. In May, 1971, this plan was expanded to afford complete off-the-job personal accident coverage as well, at a modest premium charge to the employee.

The anniversary year brought even more substantial enlargement of employee benefits, in the form of a long-term disability income plan. Starting August 1, this affords all United States and Canadian employees who may become totally disabled a guaranteed income of 60% of basic earnings at the time of disablement, up to a maximum of $1,500 per month. Noncontributory for employees earning less than $8,667 per year, the plan calls for a sliding-scale contribution from more highly-salaried staff. Payments begin six months after total disability and continue until recovery, or until normal pension benefits become payable at 65.

⚓   ⚓   ⚓

Public relations, the art (or science) of persuasive self-explanation and friend-winning so indispensable today to large corporations, public agencies, and social causes, was late in gaining respectability with what were once called the "mechanic arts," or more recently the "applied sciences." This may or may not have any bearing on the fact that the Association's first formal public relations venture was not undertaken until 1956, when the Organization Program was five years old. Another factor could have been that not until the new financial footing was established were funds available for such a luxury.

In any case, it was now decided to retain, jointly with three other insurance market organizations, the firm of Doremus & Company as public relations advisers. The most conspicuous fruit of this decision, so far as the Association was concerned, was the production of a descriptive and historical brochure, *The United States Salvage Association, Inc.* Widely distributed in 1960, this attracted attention to the Association on the part of many who had not previously known of, or understood, its work and objectives. It also gained credits in an unexpected quarter, being selected by the New York Printers Association for display at their 19th Exhibition of Printing at the Hotel Commodore in January, 1961.

By the mid-sixties, the several market organizations involved had allowed this joint arrangement to lapse, and for five years thereafter the Association undertook no public relations program on its own. At the start of its semicentennial year, however, it determined, in conjunction with the American Hull Insurance Syndicate, to resume systematic efforts to give wider exposure to its activities, findings, and goals; and again retained public relations counsel to that end.

XVII

THE THIRD FUNCTION

WHILE organization and manning had produced the most visible and dramatic changes in the Association under Thompson's management, the introduction of the Technical Section had probably been the most significant change. It was said at the start of this narrative that Association surveyors have three primary functions: physical checkup, diagnosis, and "medical" research. Until the planning of 1951 was implemented, whatever had been done under the third heading had been random, sketchy, and often wasted, because unattended by systematic assembly and collation of records, to insure the cumulative availability of research findings.

The fundamental motivation of the Technical Section, tabulation and analysis of repetitive types of vessel damage in order to reduce their frequency, and hopefully to eradicate them, has sometimes been cynically described as the Association's "working itself out of a job." Happily (or unhappily), as with most safety and health programs in other fields, there seem likely to be enough loss-productive conditions and practices in ship design, construction, and operation to last a long time. The Association and its underwriter principals know this —and have come to recognize that, with repair costs steepening, the organization's work in this field may well be its most rewarding activity, besides being its most idealistic.

After a year and a half, Thompson described the Section's progress as "most gratifying." It had by then established machinery for "detailed review of survey reports and repair costs, research, and dissemination of pertinent information to the surveying staff." In 1955, a technical library was established under the supervision of a professional librarian.

For all its initial promise, and Thompson's personal back-

HARRY S. TOWNSEND
Vice President

RICHARD D. JAESCHKE
Vice President-Operations

ASSOCIATION VICE PRESIDENTS, 1971

ing, the Technical Section had a distinct weakness in its early years: lack of continuous direction by one individual. Neither Pulliam, its first head, nor Sherman, its second, held the post for a full year. Watkins, who was named technical assistant August 1, 1953, and technical supervisor February 1, 1954, had almost continuous distracting responsibilities, notably those of New York area principal surveyor (without portfolio) from Varni's retirement in 1953 to Henry's appointment in 1956. Before the Section could realize its potential, it had to come under the sustained direction of a man who was exactly the right blend of theoretical scholar, practicing engineer, and fanatic. No one else could fully actualize the concept underlying this new activity and make it prevail over the inertial forces of tradition and "practicality." As the fifties wore to a close, it became clear that Harry S. Townsend was that man.

Townsend's appointment as technical assistant in 1954,

and technical supervisor in April, 1958, simply confirmed formally a role he was already filling on his own in the Association's routine work, experience analysis, and special studies. Among technological developments closely followed by the organization during this period were the continuing fractures of war-built welded hulls, gear failures on C4-type vessels, government construction of the nuclear ship *Savannah* and the hydrofoil ship *Denison,* and the carriage of liquefied methane ("LNG") in ocean ships. Active attention was also given to the work then in progress on developing a United States position for revision of the International Load Line Convention of 1930.

Another international activity in which the Technical Section has been of continuing service to American underwriters is compilation of material for the use of Institute delegates attending the yearly meetings of the International Union of Marine Insurance. For the 1962 meeting alone, Townsend prepared five such back-up memoranda on subjects ranging from cargo vessel subdivision and fishing boat design to the inadequacies of tonnage measurement. The ready accessibility of such authoritative and comprehensive briefing was a valuable new service of the Association to the underwriting community.

One of the cardinal principles of the Lindgren administration is that the procedures of all its·surveyors be uniform and objective, and their reports sufficiently standardized to be fully comparable for purposes of study and analysis. To this end, in 1964, Lindgren established the now-encyclopedic and unique Marine Surveying Manual, for the composition, maintenance, updating, and dissemination of which Townsend became responsible. This raised the need for improved interregional communication and led to the institution the same year of a series of Technical Letters. These have ranged over a wide field of subject matter: from revisions and interpretations of the Manual, to extracts from newly-published research work, to original memoranda embodying results of the Association's own studies. As of August 2, 1971, this effort to keep all surveyors currently informed on the state of the art and of Association practice has resulted in the issuance of 49 Technical Letters,

Two close-ups of the painful injuries suffered by the *Aimee Lykes* when she stranded in South Africa on her maiden trip, October 26, 1963 (see p. 159).

and the consequent establishment in every branch office of a body of reference material calculated to foster the elevation and unification of professional standards.

Mention has been made of the introduction early in Thompson's regime of a vessel damage coding program. A specialist was employed and a procedure formulated, but underwriter interest proved limited, and further development was deferred. In subsequent years, increasingly sophisticated data-processing equipment found general acceptance by business firms, including the Hull Syndicate and the Association. To use this equipment most efficiently in meeting Syndicate and other calls for compendious damage survey studies, the coding program was actively renewed in the late sixties. A Damage Survey Analysis Form was designed, together with a regularly updated Coding Manual and alphabetical file of Syndicate-insured vessels. Code numbers were assigned all essential data, including ships, owners, geographic areas, types of damage, and vessel parts, by entering which on the Form a punch-card record of every reported damage can be made and stored for instant retrieval.

Apart from such continuing programs, Townsend's office has involved itself in a number of special study projects over the past dozen years. Through these, using the basic formula of distilling generic weaknesses from large numbers of similar cases, it has been able to suggest substantial improvements in shipbuilding and engineering practice, thereby helping to reduce levels of repair expenditure, and to raise those of safety at sea. The outstanding project of this sort, initiated before 1960 and still continuing in certain ramifications, is the "Heavy-Weather Forward Bottom Damage" investigation and the related cargo ship hull-form study.

From several years' mass analysis of damage survey reports, Townsend became aware that one of the most prevalent types of structural injury to American vessels was indenting and other distortion of forward bottom plating and internal structure resulting from "slamming" in heavy seas. Comparable foreign-built vessels seemed generally immune to such damage. This led him to close analysis of the forebody lines of a large number of ships in each group, and to the discovery of basic architectural differences between them. While too complex to be precisely reducible to lay language, this intercontinental split in design practice had nominally resolved itself into the preponderant use in American models of vertical-sided, or "U"-shaped, forward sections; in European, of more sloping or "V"-shaped.

The persuasive if not yet entirely conclusive evidence that most American freighter hull forms were costlier than European for underwriters and shipowners ("several million dollars per year not including lost time," it was asserted) was first made public in a 1960 paper by Townsend, "Some Observations on the Shape of Ship Forebodies with Relation to Heavy Weather." So well were these and subsequent findings received, and so fully convinced of their validity was the Association, that in 1965 it published in its own name, and distributed to underwriters and shipowners, Townsend's monumental sequel, "A Series of Cargo Vessel Hull Forms," embodying the forebody configurations most likely to allow sustained speed under heavy-weather conditions without damage.

The possibility remained that those Americans who called the European designs costlier to drive through *calm* seas might be right. This was largely demonstrated to be a myth early in 1966, in comparative tests of small-scale (5-foot) towed models of a "Townsend series" hull and the United States Lines "Challenger" hull (with a "U-type" forebody), conducted in the Stevens Institute of Technology towing tank. Such interest was aroused that the Society of Naval Architects and Marine Engineers ("SNAME"), which had had a "slamming panel" for years, voted that May to arrange for large-scale (17½-foot) self-propelled model tests in the Navy's David Taylor Model Basin in Washington, D. C. The $60,000 cost of these tests was financed by contributions from the Navy, the Maritime Administration, the marine industry, SNAME, and the Association (which put in $8,850).

The results were an overwhelming vindication of the Association's conclusions; but, to remove the last trace of doubt as to smooth-water performance of the forms advocated by Townsend, it financed further tests in the Netherlands, late in 1966,

The Heavy-Weather Forward Bottom Damage Program

Horrible examples. The two upper photographs show injury sustained by a ship, one to shell plating, one to internals, solely as a result of "slamming" in the sea.

Lower: the models used in comparative tank tests at the Stevens Institute of Technology—the "Townsend Series" hull above, the "Challenger" hull below.

N.Y. Shipbuilding Corp. photo

at an additional cost of $5,000. "This was done," as later reported, "simply because it is our philosophy that any owner would be understandably reluctant to adopt hull forms which may be less conducive to forward bottom damage, but which may require more horsepower, and consequently fuel, to propel them in smooth water." Again the Townsend forms were proved at least equal "in smooth water to what has been American practice."

The climactic step was a symposium sponsored by SNAME in New York October 10, 1967, under the title "Some Effects of Hull Form on Ship Performance in a Seaway." Papers were delivered by spokesmen for the Naval Ship Research and Development Center (formerly the David Taylor Model Basin), the Stevens Institute staff, and the United States Lines Company, but the acknowledged central figure was Harry Townsend, speaking on his once-used title "A Series of Cargo Vessel Hull Forms"—the difference being that this time there was nothing hypothetical about the Association's findings.

Immediate follow-up was confessedly disappointing. Attendance at the Symposium could have been better (though the papers were all published, which was the important thing scientifically). Shipowners and shipbuilders did not ostentatiously flock to the introduction of new designs, let alone to the costly procedure of reshaping existing hulls. But the best vindication of this extended inquiry is that calls upon the Association to survey heavy-weather forward bottom damage—and related repair charges to underwriters—have begun to fall off. It has, to that extent, "worked itself out of a job." Unquestionably it will have less and less of this particular variety of survey work in the future, and in that respect will derive less revenue, while underwriters confront smaller claims from this cause and American shipping becomes correspondingly more efficient.

The answer to any insinuation of short-term business loss from such a constructive effort is that the remaining ways in which shipping can be made more efficient (and hull underwriters' losses curtailed) by similar research procedures are almost literally infinite. The value of the Association's technical program to its owners and to the nation is therefore increased, not diminished. Harry Townsend himself stated the case for continuance of the activities he has spearheaded when he said at the symposium that the Association, in this landmark instance, had espoused "the unusual philosophy of placing emphasis on the cure of a disease rather than on the income from bedside visits."

In recognition of the benefits attained by the hull-form studies, an effort was launched in 1966 to set up a yearly tax-free reserve fund for research. However, it was reported in March, 1967, that no such program was possible under existing law. Presently, therefore, any economies the Association's research may achieve on behalf of the nation's maritime and insurance establishments must be achieved on its own unassisted resources.

Directly attributable to the Association's technical and research work is the increasing frequency with which it is invited to participate in the deliberations of learned and professional groups, both private and governmental. Since Paul Thompson was asked in 1963 to address the annual Tanker Conference of the American Petroleum Institute, such invitations for Association representatives to take part in maritime symposiums and conferences have become routine. The president and vice presidents also hold membership in more than a score of shipping technical committees of national scope, a full list of which appears as an appendix to this volume.

XVIII

CASUALTIES, SINGLY AND BY THE HUNDREDS

BEHIND the tabulations, analyses, and determinations of the Technical Section lay the enormous year-in-year-out case load of the Association's offices, representatives, and surveyors. This involved surveys of all types on vessels of all classes, large and small. When it is considered that in 1970, after twelve years' decline, damage surveys performed *on large vessels alone* still totaled 2,488, it becomes clear on what ample quantitative foundations Townsend's findings rested. It is also clear that only the slimmest sampling of noteworthy disaster cases is possible in a volume of this scope.

Of collisions requiring Association attendance since the early fifties, two of the more serious occurred in 1956 almost within hail of the home office. On the foggy approaches to New York Bay, July 23, the C2 cargo ship *Fairisle* was so injured in collision with the tanker *San Jose II* as to call for beaching in Gravesend Bay. By the time she touched bottom, however, she had taken so much water that she slowly continued to heel until she lay flat on her starboard side, a constructive total loss. A scant five months later, off the tip of Governor's Island in the Upper Bay, and within two miles of John Street, the C2 *African Star* and the C1 *Alcoa Pilgrim* came together so destructively that the former had to be beached after nearly sinking in the main ship channel.

The locale of this latter disaster probably made surveyors' chores of approving salvage, towage, and repair arrangements somewhat easier than they had been five years earlier when another "star," the war-veteran C3 *Mormacstar,* was run down at anchor by the passenger liner *Del Mar* in the harbor of Santos, Brazil. Laid open in the engineroom by a gash which cut six feet into her bottom plating, the stricken ship somehow

The freighter *Fairisle* in Gravesend Bay, New York, after her 1956 collision with the *San Jose II*.

floated till help arrived by plane from New York in the person of William Watkins. Then in his second year of employment, Watkins found himself facing the unenviable tasks of unearthing enough odd plating and welding equipment, in a port without large-ship repair facilities, to hold the freighter together (though she still had literally to float on her shored engineroom bulkheads), and then of riding her on the long, rough open-sea tow to Rio de Janeiro. All in the line of duty successfully performed, but not exactly the sort of sea voyage a tourist (or an underwriter) might fancy.

The Association's preoccupation, through the fifties, with the reasons for tankers' breaking in two has already been mentioned. Generally, this had happened to American-built T2's, and it had been possible for investigators to inspect the salvaged stern sections of the *Fort Mercer,* broken apart off Cape Cod in 1952, and the *Pine Ridge,* off Hatteras in 1960. But its climactic problem of this sort was a casualty to a foreign tanker in just about the remotest part of the world from 99 John Street: the Indian Ocean off Australia's southwest corner. The ship was the Swedish-built, Italian-owned, Liberian-flag *Bridgewater,* ripped apart in violent weather January 29, 1962. Both halves miraculously stayed afloat, and all hands were rescued, but the tug *Yuna's* ensuing tow of the stern, arranged through the Association's Fremantle representative, turned into a bitter, roundabout three-week struggle. The disaster had occurred about 250 miles due west of Fremantle but, what with stormy seas, headwinds, and parted towlines, the after half was almost 360 miles northwest of that port before she began making headway toward it. The untowable bow drifted off on the equatorial current and was reported early in March a thousand miles offshore.

Groundings and strandings which tested the resourcefulness of surveyors and salvors in the early sixties included the holing of the cargo ship *Island Mail* on a submerged rock in her home waters of Puget Sound, May 29, 1961. With her side laid open under water for almost a third of her length (a rent comparably grievous to that which sank the *Titanic*), she just managed to make the beach, to undergo prolonged and costly salvage and repair. On October 9, long before these were complete, another American freighter, the *Pioneer Muse,* lost her way in the Ryukyus en route to Japan, and tried to climb a mountain on the island of Minami Daito Shima. The results were fatal to her, as the stern broke away just abaft the midship house, leaving a half-ship clinging to the steep slope. Meanwhile, Association representatives had reached the scene, only to find that their gravest problem was how to get ashore at all on the forbidding pinnacle—a feat the ship had accomplished with ease, to make herself the costliest total loss the American Hull Insurance Syndicate had yet suffered.

February 7, 1962, brought another stranding for a total loss much nearer home: at Santa Rosa Island, California. The victim was the ten-year-old C2 *Chickasaw,* bound from Yokohama to San Pedro with cargo and four passengers. The latter, with most of the crew, rode ashore by breeches buoy four days later, after hopes of refloating her were abandoned by salvors brought to the scene, at owners' request, by the Association's Los Angeles office. A tricky but successful cargo-salvage operation followed, utilizing helicopters and the salvage vessel *Salvage Chief.*

Tanker *Alva Cape* blazes from stem to stern after colliding with the *Texaco Massachusetts* (visible at right), June 16, 1966.

KILL VAN KULL HOLOCAUST

After a further fatal blast in Gravesend Bay, the *Alva Cape* is readied for burial at sea.

Jeff Blinn photo

Better fortune (though at even greater cost) attended the refloating of the fast cargo liner *Aimee Lykes,* which stranded in South Africa on her maiden voyage, October 26, 1963. Promptly attended by Association representatives, she was restored to service, but at a million-odd-dollar expense. Fortunately, as in the other strandings mentioned, no lives were lost.

As a rule Association services were not called into play in the case of sunken ships, since, lacking a "corpus delicti" for surveyors to study, underwriters paid and wrote off the total loss. However, in the case of the most spectacular ship-disappearance of modern times, when the molten sulphur carrier *Marine Sulphur Queen* failed to make port on a routine voyage from the Gulf to the Atlantic coast in February, 1963, the facilities of the organization were called into play. Its fifteen-page report on the technological problems of ship design relative to such cargoes was credited with influencing some practices in the sulphur trade and was made a part of the United States Coast Guard's casualty investigation record.

This casualty sampling of the last twenty years ends, as it began, with two collision cases, one in the Association's home port and one in remote foreign waters. But the scale of human and monetary loss is magnified, in these latest cases, almost beyond recognition. On June 16, 1966, New York harbor experienced one of its greatest disasters (and was threatened with a far greater one) when two tankers, the *Alva Cape* and the *Texaco Massachusetts,* collided in the narrow, refinery-fringed waters of the Kill Van Kull and took fire when spilled naphtha ignited, with heavy loss of life. Following heroic rescue and containment efforts by crewmen, tugboatmen, and the Coast Guard, it fell to Association personnel to attend the *Alva Cape,* which was anchored in Gravesend Bay, to be cleared of her still perilous cargo and prepared for drydocking. Despite warnings of her explosive condition, this dangerous work continued until another fatal blast convinced the authorities that the mangled but deadly hulk must be towed to sea and sunk.

The second collision occurred off the Persian Gulf and

remains an unfinished story at this writing. On September 10, 1970, the 216,821-deadweight-ton tanker *Aquarius*, one of the newest and largest vessels afloat, was in collision with the Soviet vessel *Svetlogorsk*, burst into flame, and for many hours threatened to become one of the costliest total losses in world shipping history. Fire and flooding were ultimately controlled; but no drydock nearer than Japan could handle the mammoth casualty. She was accordingly towed there (barely negotiating Malacca Strait in her damaged and laden condition), only to be denied entry to any Japanese port as a pollution hazard. She was next towed to Philippine waters for discharge out of range of populated areas, then towed back to Japan, arriving seven months after the collision. Thus far, the towage alone (which has been subject to Association approval) has covered roughly 13,000 nautical miles of ocean and cost $1.6 million. While not a total loss, the *Aquarius* seems certain to rank as one of history's largest damage claims.

Not exactly a shipping disaster, though as urgent, was an international crisis which posed a sweeping demand for Association services on December 30, 1966. This was President De Gaulle's abrupt decision to withdraw France from the North Atlantic Treaty Organization and to require immediate removal of the extensive fleet of NATO floating equipment from its long-established French storage sites at Le Pellerin, Rochefort, and La Rochelle-Pallice. A total of some eighty vessels, including tugs, cranes, refrigerator barges, floating repair shops, and deck-loaded "LCM's" and plastic and wood-hulled "J-boats," many of them stored for considerable periods, had to be moved from French waters to Southampton or Bremen on virtual overnight notice.

In an atmosphere of breakneck urgency, the Association's London office was requested by U. S. Naval Headquarters at Bremen to make all necessary inspections and to prepare all plans and towage approvals for mass evacuation of French ports. But scarcely was this tremendous project under way, with preliminary recommendations submitted and inspectors lined up to perform the myriad surveys required, when the Navy cancelled the entire requested program, January 19, on grounds

MAMMOTH IN EVERY WAY

Her after house ravaged by collision and fire, the giant *Aquarius* lies off Bandar Abbas in September, 1970, awaiting towage to Japan.

Taking charge. With three powerful tugs hauling one direction, the *Aquarius* takes a mighty sheer in another. At times *she* towed the tugs, and once broke free entirely for several days.

*Photos courtesy L. Smit &
Co.'s International
Towing Service*

TIDAL WAVE

After 1964's
Good Friday
earthquake subsided,
the fishing boats
Celtic, Unga, and *Alco*
(top to bottom) were
among the hundreds
of craft strewn about
the environs of
Seward, Alaska.

that the submitted recommendations would suffice and the whole exodus be conducted with commercial towage on a catch-as-catch-can basis. Though it took months to tie up the loose ends of commitments made and expenditures incurred (not all of which were allowed by the Navy), the Association had the wry satisfaction of having contributed to meeting the NATO crisis of 1967.

⚓   ⚓   ⚓

In a class apart from the daily routine of calls to survey individual vessels are the periodic crises in which the full resources of a branch office, or an entire area, are marshalled to cope with a widespread natural catastrophe. Under such circumstances, instead of being requested by a specific underwriter to attend a specific vessel, the Association finds itself acting to protect the interests of many underwriters, brokers, and owners who may not yet even know which vessels at interest in the devastated area have been damaged or destroyed. One conspicuous advantage of its reorganization in the fifties has been its ability to rise to a succession of grave public emergencies in the sixties.

Especially notable was the performance of the Seattle office and the Pacific district in the aftermath of Alaska's Good Friday earthquake and tidal wave in 1964. The wave worked havoc with shipping around Kodiak and virtually obliterated the port of Seward, while the quake shattered many stored vessels and extensively altered the shoreline, above water and below, in Cordova and vicinity. Knowing only that the stricken area was under martial law and virtually without communications, Captain Marinus A. Stream, Seattle resident surveyor, responded to underwriters' concern by dispatching three of his four-surveyor staff to Alaska on hours' notice. Since his fourth assistant was already in process of resigning, he thus took on himself the full burden of a five-man port area until two emergency replacements could be flown in from the New York and New Orleans offices.

The three who went north, James Raeside to Kodiak, Frank Hanson to Seward/Anchorage, and Elvin Hawley to Cordova,

163

spent up to five weeks in those areas. Their task, to track down and inspect all craft known to be insured (or what was left of them), was carried out under conditions for which uncomfortable, frustrating, and perilous are inadequate adjectives. In the latter connection, Raeside was once able to brake his hired jalopy (the best transportation the stricken town afforded) only by crashing it into a cannery building, and Hanson came close to spending a freezing spring night in the open when his rented plane was grounded by weather. Despite all obstacles, they were able to send in surveys on 158 vessels, 76 of them total losses. Insured values on the latter group and estimated repair costs to the others were almost exactly even: $1,200,000 each.

The devoted services of this trio, and of Captain Stream, were widely praised by underwriters, at whose suggestion, strongly endorsed by the president, the Association took the extraordinary step of awarding each a bonus accompanied by a resolution of thanks for having "so willingly left their homes and for an extended period of time lived and worked under the most trying circumstances in Alaska following the earthquake."

Association services on a full emergency scale were also exacted during the decade by a quartette of Gulf hurricanes with ladylike names. The only one, however, to involve such injuries to shipping, or such demands on Association manpower, as those inflicted by the Alaskan cataclysm was "Betsy," who hammered New Orleans' ships and shipyards on September 9-10, 1965. When she had blown herself out, the banks and bottom of the Mississippi were littered with vessels old, new, and unfinished. Scattered along the levee were the *Almeria Lykes* and *Zoella Lykes* and the unfinished *Ruth Lykes* and *Mason Lykes*. Lying on the bottom were the almost-completed *Genevieve Lykes* and *Letitia Lykes*. Other wreckage was everywhere.

The New Orleans office staff, headed by Gulf district principal surveyor Joseph K. Tynan, were at work before the sky cleared. Tynan's own home had been unroofed, and others of the staff had comparable personal problems. But such problems were unquestioningly accorded second priority to the general catastrophe. Although four additional surveyors were rushed in from other offices, there was work enough to keep all hands busy around the clock for several days. Urgently needed were qualified salvagers and equipment for the stranded commercial vessels, a sunken drilling rig hull, and a capsized drydock. However, the salvage vessels *Curb* and *Cable* had been preempted for recovery of naval and other wrecked government craft. Shrewdly anticipating this, Tynan had arranged, while the wind was still blowing, for his Syndicate principals and their assureds to have first call on practically every commercial tug in the port. Thanks to this foresight, the Association was able in the first few days, before regular salvage equipment was available, to carry out the refloating of one operating and two unfinished Lykes vessels, plus the drilling rig.

In the upshot, the Association dealt with 143 cases in the battered port area during the emergency. Aggregate total loss and repair costs were much higher than in the Alaskan earthquake; but were about three-fourths concentrated in the destruction of two nearly finished high-valued hulls. Otherwise the two marine calamities were of similar gravity. In view of the enormous individual sacrifice and team effort of its staff on the scene, the Association voted its second commendation and bonus in eighteen months to the ten men involved.

While the other three hurricanes brought somewhat less carnage to shipping, they were by no means gentle. "Hilda," on October 3 and 4, 1964, vented much of her fury on offshore oil-drilling rigs, damaging twenty-five and demolishing seventeen. Grim highlight was the capsizing and sinking of the $5,600,000 rig *Bluewater No. 1* in over 200 feet of water which was anything but blue. Almost five years later, August 17 and 18, 1969, when "Camille" howled ashore between New Orleans and Mobile, it was feared for a time that she would match "Betsy's" record. She did not, but her toll was far from light. Of 44 hurricane damage surveys attended by the Association, nine were on vessels at the Ingalls Shipyard and ten on ships which had gone adrift and either collided or stranded. Two were on drilling platforms, one on a submarine pipeline, and the balance on smaller commercial and oil company equipment.

"Betsy" vs. Lykes, September, 1965

aced along the Mississippi River levee after the hurricane lie (top to bottom)
e *Almeria Lykes* of the operating Lykes fleet and the new *Ruth Lykes* and
ason Lykes, which had been under construction at Avondale Shipyards. All
ree were refloated under Association auspices within a few days.

ss fortunate were the
-but-completed *Gene-*
ve Lykes and *Letitia*
kes. Torn from their
ing-out berths, they
re swept upriver to-
her until the *Letitia*
k. In the upper view
Genevieve stands sen-
el on the shelving bank
ve her sister's grave.
n after it was taken,
began to roll and fi-
ly slid to rest on top
the *Letitia* (lower).
er prolonged efforts at
vage, they still lie there
ay.

The eve of its semicentennial found the Association cleaning up after one more untidy female, "Celia," on the south Texas coast, August 3 and 4, 1970. Her most conspicuous victim to come under survey was the 550-foot bulk ship *Trade Carrier*, driven ashore near Corpus Christi and left nine-tenths on dry (or drying) land. Association men believed that, as with two of the East Gulf victims the year before, she could be recovered without the expense to underwriters of calling in professional salvors. This was accomplished by using local dredging equipment to create a basin around the ship, in which she was successfully refloated.

After Hurricane "Celia's" passing in August, 1970, the bulk vessel *Trade Carrier* was found in this predicament and restored to her element by dredging of a basin around her, arranged by the Association.

XIX

THE END AND THE BEGINNING

I F the last decade has brought a slow diminution in number of surveys, it has produced a steady increase in another Association service, approval of equipment and arrangements for trips in tow. This activity, of course, dates back to the start of the organization. Brengle remarked at the 1927 annual meeting on the frequency of such assignments and the weighty "responsibility placed upon a surveyor who is asked to pass upon the seaworthiness of" a tow, as well as the "highly gratifying" results of such work to that date.

New impetus was given by the wartime and immediate postwar activities of Captain Bull, a leader in this field. The real upswing, however, got under way simultaneously with the NASA contract, first major peacetime towage agreement with the Government. In the same year, 1960, the Military Sea Transportation Service directed all its area commanders to see that every future towage contract was subject to Association approval. The next year brought a 30% increase in towing approval activity: from 768 cases in 1960 to 997 in 1961, followed by a further 5% gain, to 1,047, in 1962.

The governmental component of this work, though important, was by no means predominant. The Association's chief principals, here as in its other activities, were underwriters and owners interested in the safe movement of tows which were, as a rule, out of the ordinary. As Watkins reported in 1962, "the majority of the tows in which the Salvage Association participates are not usual [such as] barges on scheduled runs, harbor operations, etc. The Salvage Association is called in because of the high degree of risk involved in specific situations." He went on to cite as recent examples the 11,000-mile tow of the 358-foot floating power plant *Resistance* from Portsmouth, New Hampshire, to Pusan, Korea; the transmediterranean movement of sixteen 4,000-ton concrete caissons for a Libyan tanker terminal, and several difficult transatlantic tows of high-riding, wind-catching ship midbodies constructed abroad for "jumboizing" of vessels in this country.

The next year Lindgren amplified the list, mentioning intercoastal towage approvals of a 25,000-ton sectional drydock, a San Francisco ferryboat, and the decommissioned battleship *Alabama*. Particularly exacting, and reminiscent of Bull's wartime exploits, were the 1962 arrangements for moving an entire fleet of four tugs and eleven barges from New Orleans to Lisbon. This was so organized that the whole flotilla moved in two tandem tows, with only four of the barges actually waterborne.

At the same time that it was building up this business, the Association was becoming increasingly active in survey and advisory work for the fast-growing offshore oil-drilling industry. In 1957 it had distributed a report "Gulf of Mexico Oil Drilling and Related Marine Operations," prepared by Rear Admiral Halert C. Shepheard, retired Coast Guard Chief of Merchant Marine Safety, then serving as an Association consultant. This was followed in 1962 by a special study for underwriters "reflecting engineering, meteorological, and navigational data" relative to oil drilling and drilling equipment in the Gulf.

In the same year the Association, having already made numerous surveys of drilling rigs in the marginal wetlands of the Gulf, was requested for the first time to move offshore, for condition surveys of a group of large installations in deep water. By 1965 it was sufficiently involved in such work to become an early advocate of establishing mandatory "sea lanes" or "fairways" for the mutual protection of ships and rigs in these and other coastal shelf waters now congested with both.

The diversified expertise thus acquired in long-distance towage and oil industry equipment (coupled with sporadic Arctic and sub-Arctic operations during and since the war) was all funnelled in the late sixties into one of the Association's largest special projects, the Prudhoe Bay tows. Discovery of the

The Battleship *Alabama* and the Submarine *Drum,* towed to Mobile with Association approval from the West and East Coasts, respectively, for permanent public display.

LONG TOWS
OF THE SIXTIES

A containership midbody, arriving in the Hudson after towage from Europe, to be incorporated in a "jumboized" American vessel.

"Unitized" Towing. One of the two tandem tows by which a fleet of four tugs and eleven barges was moved from New Orleans to Lisbon, with only four barges actually touching water.

Program-loaded barge of North Slope supplies and equipment leaving Seattle.
Red Stack photo

Derrick barge and tugs
waiting in pack ice off
Point Barrow.

PAC photo

Unloading operations at Prudhoe Bay.

Red Stack photo

North Slope oilfields on Alaska's Arctic Ocean coast had made it clear that even their adequate exploration, let alone their development for production, would require a sealift of unusual volume, complexity, and specialization. Bulky machinery, construction and housing materials, food and fuel—in all 73,500 tons of dry cargo and 125,000 barrels of petroleum products during the first short navigating season—had to be barged 3,270 sea miles from Seattle to Prudhoe Bay, 167 miles inside the Arctic Circle.

Loading and rigging of all tugs and barges used in this operation was subject to inspection and approval by the Association's Seattle office. Because of the brevity of the open season —and 1969 turned out to be an exceptionally bad ice year— all barges were preloaded starting early in the spring, with maximum unitization of cargo, and despatched on a carefully planned schedule so that equipment and supplies (which included the terminal facilities onto which unloading was to take place) would arrive in the right sequence. Besides approval services at Seattle and ice-damage surveys of returned tugs and barges at the close of the season, Seattle resident surveyor Stream made a one-week inspection of the operation at Prudhoe Bay in August, 1969.

The program was repeated on an enlarged scale in 1970, when the Seattle office inspected a total of 24 tows, involving 31 tugs and 47 barges. Of these vessels, 18 and 29, respectively, were surveyed for ice damage in the fall, with estimated repairs called for in excess of $1,350,000.

This and the NASA program embody the most sophisticated and demanding problems yet dealt with by the Association in the towing field. But it can even now discern greater technical challenges ahead: for example, in waterborne movements of nuclear reactor pressure vessels, on many of which approval requests have already been handled. With their enormous weights and values, as Townsend pointed out in a 1968 review, these will demand preliminary calculations, equipment preparation, and coordinated supervision on a scale unknown to early, easiergoing inspection systems, if losses which might well be catastrophic are to be guarded against.

Certainly, no tapering-off appears imminent for towage-approval business. Over its fifth decade, the Association's work of this sort has increased 63%, from 768 approvals per year to 1,252. Last year alone saw an 8½% gain. With long-distance tug-and-barge transport clearly in the ascendant, both on inland waters and on the high seas, a continuing strong demand for experienced guidance in this field seems assured.

⚓　⚓　⚓

As technical adviser and examiner for its underwriter principals, the Association is obligated to monitor new ship deliveries closely, especially in areas of rapid and dramatic change. By following the experience and misadventures of ships of novel design, it has frequently been able to warn underwriters and operators of significant defects and to recommend preventive or corrective measures. The Townsend hull form studies are a case prominently in point.

The spate of subsidized fleet-replacement in the early sixties was of technological interest chiefly in featuring a sharp advance over traditional freighter speeds and a cautious but increasing use of engineroom automation. Otherwise, it was characterized by a rather surprising lack of innovation—among other things, in hull lines and in cargo-handling arrangements, as the forward-bottom-damage record and the fact that many of the new ships soon had to be extensively rebuilt for container carriage tend to confirm. Improvements in docking and mooring equipment were also very largely ignored. Keeping abreast of ship construction developments requires participation in acceptance trials, of which Lindgren attended many, among them those of the *American Challenger* in 1962 and of the *American Rover,* second of the more highly automated "Challenger II" class, at the end of 1964.

Hoping to alert owners and underwriters to expensive weaknesses still being built into the new ships, the Association released to the technical press in 1963 an article, "General Cargo Ship Damage," in which C. J. Hamrin joined Townsend in analyzing one year's reported damages to 100 American dry-cargo vessels. By tabulating 27 categories of injury suffered

ATOMIC TOWAGE

Nuclear reactor and two steam generators, aggregating 816 tons, leaving Chattanooga for Fort Calhoun, Nebraska, on the barge *Gulf Fleet No. 181,* April 16, 1970.

Courtesy Combustion Engineering, Inc.

Boiling water nuclear reactor and closure head, aggregating 815 tons, being loaded at Memphis, Tennessee, on the barge *Paul Bunyan,* August 27, 1971, for towage to Havre-de-Grace, Maryland. *Courtesy Chicago Bridge & Iron Co.*

they showed that, out of total repair expense to these ships exceeding $3,100,000 (disregarding lost time), $728,000 was chargeable to hull damage from striking or surging alongside piers, $613,000 to heavy weather forward bottom damage. They maintained that these costliest categories of loss—over 40% of the fleet's annual repair bill—could be largely reduced or eliminated by the installation on American freighters of bow-thrusters, wire mooring winches, and stern anchors, and by the redesigning of the typical American forebody.

Container shipping was very much on the march at this same period and, with its "growing pains" efforts to standardize box sizes and fittings, occupied much attention on the part of hull underwriters and surveyors. As single-ship values approached $20,000,000 at the turn of the decade, this scrutiny was intensified. Simultaneously, even larger and more complex designs—barge-carriers acronymically designated "LASH" and "SEABEE"—emerged as the largest and costliest successors to the break-bulk cargo liner. The Association was invited to examine the first LASH vessel, the foreign-flag *Acadia Forest,* on her maiden visit to New Orleans in October, 1969, and named to conduct any damage surveys required on her barge complement.

The most radical change in any oceangoing ship type in recent years has been, however, the evolution of the 16,000-deadweight-ton T2—considered a huge ship at the end of the second world war—into the "supertanker" of 100,000 tons in the early sixties, and more recently into the "mammoth," now ranging up to 375,000, with 500,000-tonners firmly planned and million-tonners on drawing boards.

As this swift revolution in oil-carrier design and practice progressed, the Association strove, in the interest not only of underwriters but of general marine technology and safety, to keep pace. When the MSTS tanker *Mission San Francisco* was demolished in 1957 by gas explosion following a Delaware River collision, it advised the Navy on salvage costs and identification of recovered wreckage, and subsequently assisted the Secretary of the Treasury's Committee on Tanker Hazards, appointed in the aftermath of that disaster. When one of the

The 56,000-deadweight-ton *Sinclair Petrolore*, novel oil-ore "self-unloader" and one of the largest cargo ships of her day, which blew up and sank off Brazil, December 6, 1960. *Courtesy* Marine Engineering/Log

Explosion-ripped tanks of the mammoth *Kong Haakon VII*, looking forward from the bridge of the 200,000-tonner after she reached the safety of Portugal's "Lisnave" drydock, following her near-destruction in December, 1969.
Courtesy Mr. W. D. Ewart

first dual-purpose "supers," the oil-ore ship *Sinclair Petrolore,* blew up and sank off Brazil in 1960, it sought, by consultation with owners and surviving officers, to establish the reasons. It was very much involved, as has been said, in the efforts to save the then-huge *Torrey Canyon* when her 1967 stranding first demonstrated to the world the frightening capacity for environmental pollution of this new breed of ship. However, it was not until three mammoths of more than 200,000 tons each were destroyed or horribly mutilated by explosions late in 1969 that it became aware of a sinister and devastating frailty which had somehow crept into the formula for producing ever bigger and more profitable petroleum transports.

The Association had already published, in July, 1966, a statistical study entitled "Tanker Damages," categorizing damages in a one-year period to 150 ships ranging from T2 size to three vessels in excess of 100,000 tons. This was followed the next April by a review of operational and safety aspects of a dozen typical "Large Tankers" of up to 300,000 tons, with particular attention to propulsion, maneuvering, draft, and personnel factors. But neither of these treated the frailty in question, because it was not suspected for another three years. Only when the mysterious blasts which sank the *Marpessa* and crippled the *Mactra* and *Kong Haakon VII* began to be followed by a succession of similar catastrophes did it become painfully evident that something had gone very wrong in the evolution of the mammoth tanker.

The reasons for these explosions are still undetermined. It is known that some of the victims were in ballast and cleaning tanks; but this is not a sufficient explanation. The problems of explosive atmospheres under such circumstances have been recognized for decades, and standard precautionary measures have been developed which were presumably in effect at the time of these latest blasts. Their adequacy under what have heretofore been normal situations would seem to be demonstrated by the fact that it is mainly the new giants which have been hit by the current wave of explosions.

This phenomenon may relate, the Association believes, to the fact that the only really drastic change of arrangement involved in the swift growth of T2 into mammoth has been in the ratio of tank size to ship size. The oil tanks—counterparts of a freighter's cargo holds—are normally arranged from bow to stern in three longitudinal banks, one in the centerline, the others, somewhat smaller "wing tanks," along the port and starboard sides. But whereas a typical 16,000-deadweight-ton tanker of 1945 had nine tanks in the center row, a mammoth tanker of fifteen times her total capacity today may have only four or five. In other words, tank dimensions have grown at something approaching twice the rate of hull growth.

While full answers have yet to be found, the Association's studies have convinced it of the overwhelming probability that the proneness of the largest oil carriers to tank explosions is in some way a function of tank size. In its fiftieth year, with the strong support of the Hull Syndicate, whose recent loss ratio on large tankers has reached a disturbing 112%, it has urged the oil industry and national and international maritime safety agencies to give high priority to proving or disproving this probability, and to take preventive action before it causes further loss of life and enormously valuable property.

⚓   ⚓   ⚓

From supertankers to sailing ships is a long leap, historically and technologically, but no longer than the gap between the state of American hull surveying just before the establishment of Syndicate "A" and the state of the United States Salvage Association today. It is testimony to the stature it has achieved since 1921 that at the age of 49 it gave attention and service to both. On June 25 and 26, 1970, at Dársena Norte Pier 7, Buenos Aires, the 85-year-old sailing ship *Wavertree* was surveyed for towage approval, at underwriters' request, by Richard A. Cady, principal surveyor, Atlantic area. Built in 1885 at Southampton, England, as the skysail-yarder *Southgate,* this iron-hulled daughter of the clipper ships earned her way in the carrying trade until 1910, when she was crippled off Cape Horn and salvaged to serve as a storage vessel for 37 years at Punta Arenas. In 1948 she was converted to a sand barge at Buenos Aires, and there in 1968 she was found and acquired,

Nineteenth-century sailing ship *Wavertree* under tow at Buenos Aires in November, 1968, preparatory to being made ready for her 6,500-mile Association-approved tow to a New York museum berth.

Courtesy South Street Seaport Museum

as a virtually abandoned hulk, by representatives of New York's recently-established South Street Seaport Museum.

Long stripped of square-rigged top-hamper, except for the lower sections of her fore and mizzenmasts, she was drydocked, patched, and made fit for towage north. Armed with the Association's approval, she cleared the Rio de la Plata July 3, 1970, in tow of the tug *Titan*. Thirty-three days and 6,512 nautical miles later she was safely delivered at New York, where she now occupies a berth of honor at the foot of Fulton Street.

Thus, by a survey which was both job assignment and symbolic gesture, the organization linked its present to a kind of shipping which, though already dying when it was incorporated, had been the school in which some of its earliest surveyors, notably George Bull, had taken their first courses in ship structure and maintenance. In stressing that link, the United States Salvage Association gave added significance and dimension to its own role in the still-evolving technology of the sea.

APPENDICES

SENIOR EXECUTIVE OFFICERS, 1921-1971

Years	President	Vice President	Manager or General Manager
	(Syndicate "A" and United States Salvage Association, Inc.)		
1921	Benjamin Rush	Walter W. Parsons	Charles R. Page
1922	"	"	Lawrence J. Brengle
1923-1924	Walter W. Parsons	William R. Hedge	"
1925-1926	William R. Hedge	Charles R. Page	"
1927	Charles R. Page	William H. McGee	"
1928-1929	William H. McGee	Samuel D. McComb	"
1930-1931	Samuel D. McComb	Garry C. House	Richard D. Gatewood
1932-1933	Walter W. Parsons		Lawrence J. Brengle
1934-1935	Henry H. Reed	Frederick B. McBride	"
1936	"	"	Michael F. McAlinden
1937	Frederick B. McBride	William D. Winter	"
1938-1940	W. Bradford Harwood	"	"
1941	"	William R. Hedge	"
1942-1943	"	Samuel D. McComb	None
	(United States Salvage Association, Inc.)		
1943	W. Bradford Harwood	Samuel D. McComb	None
1944-1945	"	Donald C. Bowersock	"
1946	"	Martin W. Morron	"
1947-1948	"	John S. Gilbertson	"
1949	"	Leslie J. Haefner	"
1950	"	J. Arthur Bogardus	"
1951-1952	Clifford G. Cornwell	John T. Byrne	J. Paul Thompson
1953-1954	"	Frank B. Zeller	"
1955	"	Percy Chubb, II	"
1956-1957	"	Miles F. York	"

Years	Chairman	Vice Chairman	President
1958-1959	Clifford G. Cornwell	Harold Jackson	J. Paul Thompson
1960-1961	"	Robert R. Dwelly	"
1962-1963	"	Gilbert B. Oxford	"
1964-1965	"	Walter R. Gherardi	John R. Lindgren
1966-1967	"	William R. McBean	"
1968-1969	"	G. Doane McCarthy	"
1970	"	George H. Bunyan	"
1971	Allen E. Schumacher	"	"

181

PRINCIPAL SURVEYORS

AND SENIOR HEADQUARTERS STAFF

UNITED STATES SALVAGE ASSOCIATION, INC.

1971

ROBERT E. GROSS
Principal Surveyor, European Area

RALPH G. WHITELAW
Principal Surveyor, Far East Area

RICHARD A. CADY
Principal Surveyor, Atlantic Area

ROBERT W. LEES
Principal Surveyor, Pacific Area

JAMES F. KANAPAUX
Principal Surveyor, Gulf Area

PETER S. ODIN
Principal Surveyor, Great Lakes Area

CHARLES S. ROBERTS
Principal Surveyor, Survey Reports

THOMAS A. SMITH
Assistant Principal Surveyor,
Survey Reports

THOMAS F. WALSH
Chief, Evaluation and Repair Cost

JOHN R. McINTYRE
Navigation

GEORGE J. WILDERS
Estimator

ANDREW FLETCHER, JR.
Fleet Analysis

OFFICER AND BRANCH OFFICE STRUCTURE
UNITED STATES SALVAGE ASSOCIATION, INC.
1971

The executive structure of the United States Salvage Association today falls into two categories: individuals elected or appointed to the headquarters and executive office staff in New York, and field surveyors in charge of areas or exclusive branch offices.

Heading the first group is Allen E. Schumacher, chairman of the Board of Directors. Managerial direction of the executive office, and of the Association as a whole, is vested in the president, John R. Lindgren. He is currently assisted by Harry S. Townsend, vice president, and by Richard D. Jaeschke, vice president—operations. Other general officers are George H. Bunyan, vice chairman of the board, and Robert T. Luehman, secretary-treasurer. Until the 1971 annual meeting, and hence until the fiftieth anniversary of the Association's incorporation, the secretaryship was held by S. Donald Livingston who, by virtue of having been first elected in 1944, holds the distinction of having served longer in a single office than any other executive in the history of the Association.

Branch offices maintained in the Association's exclusive interest, under the direction of resident surveyors, now number 22, and are grouped under the regional jurisdiction of four North American and two overseas areas. Area chiefs bear the title principal surveyor. Areas, offices, and the surveyors in charge are listed on the next page.

There are presently 88 representatives holding Association appointments in over 100 foreign and two U. S. ports. Broadly, jurisdiction is allocated as follows: *New York*—Western Hemisphere, South Africa, India, Australia, Oceania; *London*—Europe, North Africa, the Near East; *Yokohama*—Japan, East and Southeast Asia, the Philippines.

Area	Branch Office	Principal or Resident Surveyor
Atlantic		Richard A. Cady
	Boston, Massachusetts	Elvin C. Hawley
	New York, New York	Richard A. Cady
	Philadelphia, Pennsylvania	Joseph A. Woods
	Baltimore, Maryland	Andrew Pierce
	Norfolk, Virginia	Alton P. Hockaday
	Jacksonville, Florida	David E. Swan
	Miami, Florida	Donald G. Ford
Gulf		James F. Kanapaux
	Mobile, Alabama	Winton T. Ames
	New Orleans, Louisiana	James F. Kanapaux
	Beaumont, Texas	Avon Dale Shaw
	Houston, Texas	Joseph P. Clayton
Great Lakes		Peter S. Odin
	Cleveland, Ohio	Peter S. Odin
	Chicago, Illinois	Amos M. Bagley
Pacific		Robert W. Lees
	Wilmington, California	Thomas Goedewaagen
	San Francisco, California	Charles W. McAuliffe
	Portland, Oregon	Earl R. Rovig
	Seattle, Washington	Marinus E. Stream
	Honolulu, Hawaii	Perry R. Kornegay, Jr.
	Vancouver, British Columbia (as Marine Surveyors of Western Canada)	John Kennedy
European		Robert E. Gross
	London, England	Robert E. Gross
	Rotterdam, Holland	J. H. W. Van Aalst
Far East		Ralph G. Whitelaw
	Yokohama, Japan	Yuan Chen

PUBLIC AND INDUSTRY COMMITTEES ON WHICH THE ASSOCIATION IS NOW OR HAS RECENTLY BEEN REPRESENTED

United States Government advisory groups:
    Shipping Coordinating Committee
    United States Load Line Committee
    United States SOLAS Working Group on Subdivision and Stability
    United States SOLAS Working Group on Safety of Fishing Vessels
American Boat and Yacht Council Committee
American Bureau of Shipping
    Membership in the Bureau
    Special Committee on Ship Operations
American Institute of Marine Underwriters
    Container Technical Subcommittee
    Hull Loss Prevention Committee
    Salvage Award Committee
National Academy of Sciences
    Ship Structure Reliability Analysis Committee
    Slamming Studies Committee
    Ad Hoc Panel on Ship Design as Related to Ship Safety
National Fire Protection Association
    Committee on Marine Fire Protection
    Sectional Committee on Gas Hazards
    Sectional Committee on Motor Craft
    Sectional Committee on Shipbuilding, Repair and Lay-up
Society of Naval Architects and Marine Engineers
    Marine Technology Committee
    Slamming Panel
    Panel on Design Procedure and Philosophy
    Two Ad Hoc Hydrodynamic Panels
Underwriters' Laboratories Marine Committee

INDEX

(Italic page numbers indicate illustrations)

193

(Illustrations without credit lines are from Association files)